D1207597

MAKING SENSE TOGETHER

MAKING SENSE TOGETHER

AN INTRODUCTION TO WILD SOCIOLOGY

John O'Neill

Harper & Row, Publishers
New York, Evanston, San Francisco, London

MAKING SENSE TOGETHER: AN INTRODUCTION TO WILD SOCIOLOGY

 For information address Harper & Row, Publishers, Inc., 10 East 53d Street, New York, N.Y. 10022. Published simultaneously in Canada by Fitzhenry & Whiteside Limited, Toronto.

LIBRARY OF CONGRESS CATALOG CARD NUMBER: 74–4861

STANDARD BOOK NUMBER: 06–131841–8 (PAPERBACK)

STANDARD BOOK NUMBER: 06–136162–3 (HARDCOVER)

Designed by Ann Scrimgeour

For Maria
A promise of sundays

Contents

You see, Sir, that in this enlightened age I am bold enough to confess that we are generally men of untaught feelings, that, instead of casting away all our old prejudices, we cherish them to a very considerable degree, and, to take more shame to ourselves, we cherish them because they are prejudices; and the longer they have lasted and the more generally they have prevailed, the more we cherish them. We are afraid to put men to live and trade each on his own private stock of reason, because we suspect that this stock in each man is small, and that the individuals would do better to avail themselves of the general bank and capital of nations and of ages. Many of our men of speculation, instead of exploding general prejudices, employ their sagacity to discover the latent wisdom which prevails in them. If they find what they seek, and they seldom fail, they think it more wise to continue the prejudice, with the reason involved, than to cast away the coat of prejudice and to leave nothing but the naked reason; because prejudice, with its reason, has a motive to give action to that reason, and an affection which will give it permanence. Prejudice is of ready application in the emergency; it previously engages the mind in a steady course of wisdom and virtue and does not leave the man hesitating in the moment of decision skeptical, puzzled, and unresolved. Prejudice renders a man's virtue his habit, and not a series of unconnected acts. Through just prejudice, his duty becomes a part of his nature.

—Edmund Burke.

MAKING SENSE TOGETHER

1
Approach

Every approach needs to presume upon its reception. And, so, in beginning we never fear that we shall be wholly misunderstood; we trust that our hesitancy, our stumbling talk, and our choice of words are not a search in the dark. To begin is confidently part of the work of building and sharing an understanding. It is ideally the institution of making sense together within a common life and a common world.

Any approach asks for an understanding. In this sense our approach is never just a casual opening, any more than the opening of a Platonic dialogue or the break of dawn is irrelevant to the experiences that are to follow. An opening is never just a beginning except in retrospect. We begin in the midst of things, that is to say, when it is already late and we are caught irrevocably in the web of understandings, borrowed back and forth against the time we have spent together—in thought, in work, in play, in love or in hate.

Our approach is self-consciously a presentation: the presence of others and of ourselves to them. Thus it is **we** who are latently the resource and circumstance that permits us to choose our ground, to start here rather than there, to abide and concede, to question and answer. And we would never get under way were it not for a certain surrender to the tide of presence, the invitation of a look, or of a word that launches us on a voyage of meaning and truth in which each will have different tasks and different dreams, yet all come safely to the shore. For such a voyage the irresistible call is that of truth to which we must fit our talk and all it involves; just as we fit out our ships, not knowing everything they will encounter but trusting everything men have learned from the sea to build into themselves and into their ships in order to sail. In this enterprise we can be confident of ourselves only in the chain of work. We have not to start from the posture of loneliness, nor amidst any babel of tongues. This does not mean that we may not in search of truth keep lonely watch or fall upon exotic islands and strange sights. Yet all these things can be told in our tales, which are somehow suited to bringing back and keeping memory for the telling of things unseen and deeds unheard.

Nor can we set out until we are ready; and thus our voyage begins at home in the world of familiar objects, among friends and everyday scenes. We cannot take our leave without a word or a smile; without checking the ropes, our trusty knife, the matches, the salt, the back door, the tickets, and the passports. Whether we leave for the Orient, the cottage, or the moon, we do not expect to encounter a totally alien scheme of things. We take along toothpaste, a clean shirt, and everyone's best wishes for our new life, whether in marriage or in Canada. We remember all we have been told by friends, novelists, poets, wise men, and even science-fiction writers. We never go alone; we are always ambassadors, representatives of the people, missionaries, or anthropologists.

And something of the sort must be true. Or else by what right do we leave home and friends? By what right do we exchange day and night and wander into regions where our own language and customs become self-conscious, strained, and perhaps unusable? What is it that drives us to know more, or to know anything else than what those around us know, those who have always known us and loved us and never thought we would leave or want anything else than what we had between us? For this is a difference at the heart of things, greater than all the variations of man and woman, of childhood and maturity, of race or class or history. Once we no longer believe that all knowings and misunderstandings and all loves or hates lie within the same flesh and fold of humanity, we do not simply invite the philosopher's loneliness, we suffer the agony and ridicule of solipsism. This is not just to think bravely on one's own, as it might seem to be, but a betrayal of the bond between us and man that, for all it has cost him, God himself has never wholly broken. We shall have to deal with the temptations of solipsism, but not as a beginning. First we must make our preparations for leaving. For then the bustle of getting ready pushes loneliness into a sentiment of things to come, an adventure within our journey rather than the ground from which we start.

To begin is to approach our work; to be alone is to be at work. Yet we must remember the variety and seasons of work to understand its common load. We must remember the terraced vineyards, the railroads, and the docks; we must not forget the insides of factories, mines, and ships; we must be able to hear the roar of trucks, the screech of sawmills. We must feel the fisherman's cold, the weight of things, how they tear and waste those who work them. But if we wish to start right, it is not enough to remember these things in a casual glance, the way we might thumb through an atlas. We must think of the joys of labor as well as its pains, its celebration in things as well as its struggle with them. We must know what it is people do in their work, how they feel, what they see, what they hear, what they need from steel, or marble, or bread; and how all this is metamorphosed into everyday life and in the simplest exchange between us, in friendship, in families, in love, in fear, in anxiety, and in cruelty, in strikes and reconciliations.

In approaching our own task of making sense together, we naturally reach backward and forward, and in this we heighten our sense of commitment to the commonplaces of meaning, habit, and community to which we have been accustomed. For years now I have read and talked and studied. I have written books and critical papers. I have attended conferences and discussions, quarreled over methodologies and relevances, and taken sides. I have been persuaded as well as persuasive. I have learned how to lecture, to give a talk, to chat, to amuse and cajole, to criticize and anger. On every occasion I needed an audience as much as I was needed by them. And yet this exchange hides all that went into the years in which I learned to make an audience what it wanted to be and to find in the audience what I could not find in myself. I needed them because of a simple conviction that the sense of things is not alien and that knowledge and truth have only messengers and no experts. Truth has a face: it is the work of man and earns his bread. Thus in the work of knowledge we intend only to open paths that others can follow. Messengers, of course, carry news that they do not know will be well received in the community. But at first they are made welcome, brought in from the cold and rain, given food and drink and a place to rest from their journey. And it is the same when we get our news from the morning paper over a cup of coffee. We think of the truth as part of the well-being of our community; we receive it as sustenance, or as a friend or guest. That is why the truth is painful when it reveals that things are not well in the land, in our lives, or in our community.

To begin a work is to solicit an encounter between ourselves and others present to us here and now, or through their work and its legacy. Such a beginning is of the order of intimacy and revelation in which we discover a primitive sense of closeness. Yet our approach would be unbearable if it were not like the meeting of eyes in which there can be no primacy of the self or of the other but only a kind of alternating life. Our approach is rather an invitation to friendship and love, unsure yet certain. It is a warm embrace in which we are caught up in that overlap in which we spend our lives together and which invites comparison and understanding as much as fear or uncertainty. This is the ground for starting with one another. The encounter with someone or something new to us awakens in us a sense of openness, the sharing of need, that provides the horizon to our own vocation and is prior to all motivations of love, anonymity, creativity, or destruction. In this sense the encounter with beginnings, or first times, is not a radical break with everyday life. It is like a breath we draw more deeply at first and then let go, just as the fullness of life may rush in upon us and then recede, returning us to the ordinary absorption of living. This encounter of first things is both a nostalgia and an ideal to which we compare our everyday experience without willfully courting either terror or ennui, yet not without longing and yearning.

> We are talking now of summer evenings in Knoxville, Tennessee, in the time that I lived there so successfully disguised to myself as a child. . . .
>
> . . . All my people are larger bodies than mine, quiet, with voices gentle and meaningless like the voices of sleeping birds. One is an artist, he is living at home. One is a musician, she is living at home. One is my mother who is good to me. One is my father who is good to me. By some chance, here they are, all on this earth; and who shall even tell the sorrow of being on this earth, lying, on quilts, on the grass, on a summer evening, among the sounds of night. May God bless my people, my uncle, my aunt, my mother, my good father, oh, remember them kindly in their time of trouble; and in the hour of their taking away.
>
> After a little I am taken in and put to bed. Sleep, soft smiling, draws me unto her: and those receive me, who quietly treat me

> as one familiar and well beloved in that home: but will not, oh, will not, not now, not ever; but will not ever tell me who I am.[1]

There is a kind of sufficiency to things in which they realize themselves, neither falling short nor exceeding their limits. Here we have begun the enterprise of exploring our need of one another, thereby making thematic something we always assumed. We are engaged in an exercise that will involve us in mentioning what might never need to have been said and in falling short, or rather falling back into that embrace that surpasses all reason. Our task then is one of memory, of the care of first and last things, and in this the world and those around us are our support. We wish to understand and love one another, to be understood by others and by ourselves. We look about for certainties and find the memory of a summer evening on the grass among our family invading us with the presence that comes in the weight and lift of our bodies, in the sight and sound of our brother and sister and the goodness of our mother and father. And we borrow our own presence from theirs who in all the comings and goings of their own lives are here with us this evening and dwell in our heart by a marvelous chance of warmth and love. These are arrangements that are lasting like a family that lasts against its own troubles and dyings, as summer evenings last all the while that they, too, are dying. It is certain that we are not deceived in these familiar memories and do belong to them. Yet in the slip of time we do not hold and so become a question to ourselves, even while those around us still care and treat us as one so well loved and known to them, but who will not now or ever tell us who we are. And who can ever forget the places of memory?

We need to understand what moves us, what it is in the way a table is set, a garden cared for, or the way a mother dresses

1. James Agee, **A Death in the Family** (New York: Bantam Books, 1969), pp. 11, 14.

her child, that holds us and makes us either cry or sing somehow to tell about it—to hold it against time, against profusion, against our own indifferences or the times we are not watchful. In part this is what we can mean by simplicity, that is to say, a way of allowing ourselves to be the occasion of the fullness of things, of the world, of man. For the rest, it is the transcendence or transfiguration of things through us that is love's union of the mind and heart in love's thought **(amor intellectualis).**[2] What I have in mind here is the "world-building" character of love that makes its objects absolutely necessary, sometimes in themselves but also altogether, so that we feel we shall burst with the world inside us. Not everyone knows this feeling; or rather, it is rarely a beginning. For many, the world is in pieces; analysis is their soul or else a methodology of indifference that separates and reduces the world so pitifully that a man can empty the world.

It is sometimes thought that the thinker is a man without passions, a homeless figure. But this is false to the passionate understanding that is the very circumstance of things; it is false to the world that the thinker beholds and moreover shares in principle, though for want of company he may appear to hoard his love.[3]

Since Descartes we have been persuaded that a solitary and sedentary thinker could achieve certain and public knowledge of the world. The price of such subjective certainty, namely, the split between mind and nature, including the thinker's own embodiment, has been considered "proper" to thinking. Indeed, insofar as embodiment enters thinking or the effort to think, it

2. M. C. D'Arcy, S.J., **The Mind and Heart of Love: Lion and Unicorn: A Study in Eros and Agape** (Cleveland and New York: The World Publishing Company, Meridian Books, 1956).

3. Soren Kierkegaard, **Concluding Unscientific Postscript,** trans. David F. Swenson and Walter Lowrie (Princeton, N.J.: Princeton University Press, 1941), bk. 2, chap. 3, sec. 4, "The Subjective Thinker: His Task, His Form, His Style."

has been only as something to be put out of play. The techniques of disembodied thinking have varied from closing one's eyes in order to shut out the fleeting world of the senses, or raising one's eyes toward heaven in thought or prayer, in order at least to be in the right way of what is noble and abiding, not to mention the practice of more ascetic spiritual disciplines of the body and soul. These gestural and postural choreographies of thought, to which must be added a number of other seclusive devices, such as the study cell lined only with the silent voices of the past, or the habit of working at night when the world shuts down and the senses in particular are handicapped, run deeper than the behavioral quirks of philosophers. For all kinds of work result in a certain physiognomy, in the peasant's bent back, the waitress's varicose veins, the heavy shoulders of the truck driver. Indeed, certain kinds of work, such as surgery, piano playing, tightrope and high wire walking, are essentially body work and as such demand a regime that can no more be reduced to a technique than can thinking in the true philosopher. The activities of the body, whether proper to such work as that of the acrobat, or apparently circumstantial, as in the work of the philosopher, cannot be reduced to a lower order, except as a metaphysical posture—as the determination to redeem nature, or to dominate it by means of an ascesis.

Once we understand the world-building nature of love, we can make sociological thinking a daily practice that does not isolate us before things or them before us—which is the favorite mode of contemplation—but is instead beholden to the scenes in which we live, in streets, in gatherings, in labors, in ways and customs. In other words, we shall understand love's thought as a mode of everyday care. In addition, we can see that it is ordinarily improper to separate knowledge and morals. For we do not look upon things indifferently but rather for the goodness that is in them; and we measure our own maturity by what it is we can appreciate in this life. In this sense, then, the simplest heart is the most learned; for it knows how to take account of the ways of things and of people in their ways.

What is the direction of such thinking? To some it will be quite beside the concern with the accumulation of sociological knowledge and the domination of the world. To others it will seem to ignore the hierarchy of being and concern that has been the essence of philosophical thought. Well, this thinking, like love itself, does not move out of the plenitude in which it finds itself; it dwells in a concern with the things and people around us. Such thought does not treat its circumstances as a background for its own act; it does not abstract from its circumstances, rising above them. I do not mean, however, that we cannot learn to think heroically, forever leaving the land of circumstance and the place of everyday cares. But then the hero dies young, for there is nothing to age him, nor anyone whose ways borrow from his life so that he and they grow older together. Today, more than ever, we need to cultivate what is near to us, to make of thought a garden rather than a bypass or a perishable collection that can only land us on the moon. Such a retreat would not weaken the universality of sociological thought. "We must try to find for our circumstance, such as it is, and precisely in its very limitation and peculiarity, its appropriate place in the immense perspective of the world. We must not stop in perpetual ecstasy before hieratic values, but conquer the right place among them for our individual life. In short, the reabsorption of circumstance is the concrete destiny of man."[4]

We make our lives from what is around us, from our family, our house, street, playmates, school, teachers, friends, books, comics, and church. But we forget this. Our projects take us away from home; they sweep everything behind us as a past we

4. José Ortega y Gasset, **Meditations on Quixote,** trans. Evelyn Rugg and Diego Marin (New York: W. W. Norton & Co, 1961), p. 45.

hardly remember. We move on, looking for wider perspectives, new experiences, unseen things. Our thoughts destine us for utopia and in this we are for a time heroic figures, resisting the inertia of things, giving them our own extraordinary accent. But things beckon us back—the weight of things, their touch, their smell; the time of things, their seasons; the way of things, their uses—all these offer us a chance of salvation, a redemption rooted in things, often comically, but in an ultimate wisdom. For the truth of the life-world is that the way of things is the way of ourselves with them, like the friendship of a man and his dog —a bond of faith, a mutual need, each unthinkable apart from the other, even in argument and anger.

To think sociologically is to dwell upon a question we have answered long ago: How it is that men belong to one another despite all differences? This is the task of a **wild sociology,** namely, to dwell upon the platitudes of convention, prejudice, place, and love; to make of them a history of the world's labor and to root sociology in the care of the circumstance and particulars that shape the divine predicaments of ordinary men.[5] The work of sociology, then, is to confront the passionless world of science with the epiphany of family, of habit, and of human folly, outside of which there is no remedy. This is not to deny scientific sociology. It is simply to treat it as a possibility that has yet to convince the world. Wild sociology is mindful of the poverty of sociology, of its ambitions and its easy alliances. It sees no other way than to remain in the world it needs for its own vocation and for the particulars of its reasoning. It has no unprecedented claims, and its meditations draw ever deeply

5. "The essential is to describe the vertical or wild Being as that pre-Spiritual milieu without which nothing is thinkable, not even the spirit, and by which we pass into one another, and ourselves into ourselves in order to have **our own** time." Maurice Merleau-Ponty, **The Visible and the Invisible,** ed. Claude Lefort, trans. Alphonso Lingis (Evanston, Ill.: Northwestern University Press, 1968), p. 204.

from the very ground they seem to make strange. Wild sociology exhibits without end its appeal to the ancestral orders of our everyday conventions. Yet this does not mean that sociological thinking lacks any election. It simply means that the vocation of sociology is never in hand as a hard and fast beginning but is to be found over its way and through its concerns. It is therefore never reducible to a matrix of procedural rules. The success of wild sociology lies in the integrity of its concerns and not in the division of its labor.

Our approach to sociology cannot be hasty with the imperatives of science if we are ever to know its worth. What is the necessity of sociology, in what need do we stand of its particular concern? This is a question of fulfillment, like asking someone we love what it is they are doing so as to bring their labor closer to us than our very eyes because we want to take it in and hold it to our heart. Wild sociology cannot be self-serving. Nor should it borrow from others mindlessly. Either way, we accumulate with nothing to call our own. We need to start conscious of others, willing to learn, to be overwhelmed, to struggle, to fight back, and to stand. But this is a time of waiting even when it hides itself as worldly success. True growth needs origins, a return to first things, to place, time, and pattern. Intellectual order is not simply an instrument of domination; it involves just as much a capacity for reliving our thoughts. It is perhaps more like housecleaning, a rearrangement that in welcoming others leaves more room for ourselves. In such welcome there is a yield of being that is achieved in the arrangement of simple things to do honor to one like ourselves. The integrity of our beginnings is the source of our welcome. It also strengthens our speech and the commitment of our interests and thereby reminds us of our freedom. For in thinking and speaking we choose paths much as in life we choose careers and marriages, that is, as ways of resolving the history and geography of our lives.

The language and history of sociology may seem far removed from all this. It is, indeed, if we think of our approach to sociology as an initiation into a logic of generalization and precision to which we have no native claim. But it is just this way into sociology of which I do not want to take advantage; I do not want to settle before I begin the question of the relation of scientific languages to everyday speech and talk. I have begun by trying to show a concern for how it is we manage any departure together, how we approach understanding building upon the great platitudes of our experience as embodied beings, with our speech set in local needs and circumstances. To say that we are sociologists is only to remark on the materials at hand, upon the necessity of working on this rather than that. We must first raise the question of what it is that is presupposed by the field we have chosen to work. The practice of sociology, like any other discipline, is precarious. It soon leaves us unable to remember our first motives for doing it at all. The aim of method, as I understand it, is to test in us that strange distance between our work and those for whom we intend it. Sociologists are particularly attached to methods for the sake of their claim to scientific status; I am concerned with the poetic claims of method. I think these two belong together in our working lives. Method plays the music in what is of interest to us; it shapes our sensibilities, determines our passions, and defines our world. Method is our practical idealism; it is the opening in things and of ourselves toward them. This is possible because we are able to convert our private enthusiasms into objective enterprises that, in turn, are never accomplished once and for all and so require of us a constant response according to our own need.

Finally, in what follows, I have adopted the commonplace method, as I understand it. The notes and texts upon which I have relied, whether shown for themselves or through my own reflection, are intended as places of embellishment. Their work is to celebrate the world's own appeal rather than to defend the authority of science. They are copied as holy works seeking the redemptions of correct spelling in the salvation of divine and human reading.[6]

6. Cassiodorus Senator, **An Introduction to Divine and Human Readings,** trans. Leslie Webber Jones (New York: Octagon Books, 1966), p. 133.

2
The Conversation of Mankind

So much of language was poetry before it became prose, and still today not much of "ordinary language" is prose however different it is, and it is not much different from poetry.[1] Indeed, in the everyday language of children and adults, for they are often to be found together, poetry continues to be a power not only over words and thoughts but also over things and behavior. Therefore, like Vico we believe poetry is essential to our living and is not to be overlooked by wild sociologists. Or, at least, poetry cannot be overlooked by sociologists once we do not begin with the assumption that our speech is governed by language in its literal, or scientific, form. It is time for sociology to consider how it means to connect language and reason once it sheds the outworn conception of science and poetry as two hostile knowings. We are aware, of course, that societies vary

1. Maurice Merleau-Ponty, **The Prose of the World,** ed. Claude Lefort, trans. John O'Neill (Evanston, Ill.: Northwestern University Press, 1973); **The New Science of Giambattista Vico,** trans. from the 3d ed. (1744) by Thomas Goddard Bergin and Max Harold Fisch, revised and abridged (Ithaca, N.Y., and London: Cornell University Press, 1970).

in the respect they accord to the works of knowledge and imagination. What we know of this makes it conventional for sociology to aspire to the status of scientific knowledge and thus to shun the fall into poetry as a failure of power and control. Because we know this we need to find out that, all along, this organization of knowledge and language has been a conventional arrangement and that other visions have gathered around it, if not inside.[2]

We should not overlook the attractive power and pride of science, its ability to keep ranks and well-ordered speech. In comparison, other knowledge is a poor thing and common sense sounds like the babble of children and elders or of the scrambled wits of the careerless. Yet we know very well that language is not all of a piece. We know this because we know that ordinary men are neither obsessed nor privileged with a single vision. Language is not outside the variety of human conditions. The generalities men care for are more like the hills and valleys they see around them, more like the fates of their children, their animals, and homes, than the high-sounding generalizations of science and mathematics—more like prayer and poetry. But then sociology ought to exercise care in its own speech, since it cannot presume upon its scientific allegiances to hold it in faith with its proper place in men's lives.

The sociologist's speech is not separable from his manner of speaking, for sociology accumulates no determinate body of

2. Elizabeth Sewell, **The Orphic Voice: Poetry and Natural History** (New Haven, Conn.: Yale University Press, 1960); Michael Polyani, **Personal Knowledge: Towards a Post-Critical Philosophy** (Chicago: University of Chicago Press, 1958); **Intellect and Hope: Essays in the Thought of Michael Polyani,** ed. Thomas A. Langford and William H. Poteat (Durham, N.C.: Duke University Press, 1968); Hans Jonas, **The Phenomenon of Life: Toward a Philosophical Biology** (New York: Dell Publishing Co., 1966); Erwin Strauss, **The Primary World of the Senses: A Vindication of Sensory Experience,** trans. Jacob Needleman (New York: The Free Press of Glencoe, 1963); Maurice Merleau-Ponty, **Phenomenology of Perception,** trans. Colin Smith (London: Routledge and Kegan Paul; New York: Humanities Press, 1962).

knowledge outside the need of society to be persuaded of its use. To the extent that the sociologist is forgetful of this dependence, he speaks to himself only. But this is the source of his pride. Such pride may comfort the sociologist in his distance from the daily conversation of mankind. This attitude is more likely due to the sociologist's loss of ability to handle the tension between what is urgent and what is easy in everyday life. Yet to live with this tension is the mark of ordinary maturity. Fortunately, nothing preserves sociological speech from foolishness and banality once its content is known. Nothing is more vain than a sociology whose content cannot be found except as the promise of science. Yet the sociologist cannot wholly avoid these dangers if he is to respect common sense while nevertheless urging its improvement.

The sociologist is in danger of speaking as though only scientific utterances were true to the practical bearing of life. Rather, sociology fosters the practicality of life in order to make of itself a scientific exemplar. Yet because of the necessity of making himself heard among the other voices of science, history, and economics, the sociologist seeks to persuade common sense that the spirit of science lies in the voice of inquiry and discussion, thereby allowing for the possibility of his own place in the conversation of mankind. This is an insidious argument. For once it is admitted, it easily serves the usurpation of genuinely different modes of discussion by the high-sounding voice of expertise. Yet sociology, more than any other voice, should be concerned with the preservation of that meeting place of mankind for which Michael Oakeshott has so marvelously furnished us with the image of conversation rather than of inquiry or argument.

> This, I believe, is the appropriate image of human intercourse —appropriate because it recognizes the qualities, the diversities, and the proper relationships of human utterances. As civilized human beings, we are the inheritors, neither of an inquiry

> about ourselves and the world, nor of an accumulating body of information, but of a conversation, begun in the primeval forests and extended and made more articulate in the course of centuries. It is a conversation which goes on both in public and within each of ourselves. Of course there is argument and inquiry and information, but wherever these are profitable they are to be recognized as passages in this conversation, and perhaps they are not the most captivating of the passages. It is the ability to participate in this conversation, and not the ability to reason cogently, to make discoveries about the world, or to contrive a better world, which distinguishes the human being from the animal and the civilized man from the barbarian. Indeed, it seems not improbable that it was the engagement in this conversation (where talk is without a conclusion) that gave us our present appearance, man being descended from a race of apes who sat in talk so long and so late that they wore out their tails. Education, properly speaking, is an initiation into the skill and partnership of this conversation in which we learn to recognize the voices, to distinguish the proper occasions of utterance, and in which we acquire the intellectual and moral habits appropriate to conversation. And it is this conversation which, in the end, gives place and character to every human activity and utterance. I say, "in the end," because, of course, the immediate field of moral activity is the world of practical enterprise, and intellectual achievement appears, in the first place, within each of the various universes of discourse; but good behaviour is what it is with us because practical enterprise is recognized not as an isolated activity but as a partner in a conversation, and the final measure of intellectual achievements is in terms of its contribution to the conversation in which all universes of discourse meet.[3]

Science, common sense, and poetry are varieties of language rather than declensions of controlled communication. Man does not always seek things poetically. He may equally seek to dominate things, to subject them to his will and control, to construct them. In this case, the presence of things recedes in favor of their analytic composition, which together with their

3. Michael Oakeshott, "The Voice of Poetry in the Conversation of Mankind," in his **Rationalism in Politics and Other Essays** (London: Methuen & Co., 1962), p. 199.

laws of combination permits man's assembly of the world. Or else things are subject to traditional use and need, and concern us only insofar as they serve our purposes. Language is anchored upon ourselves, our relations to others, to God and nature, and in the history and stories that accumulate in our communities. Our care for language shapes our responsibility to ourselves and others; it is the mark of our faithfulness to the nature of things, to their shape and drift. Our use of language is not ruled by the scandals of philosophy and science. Yet its patient task of shaping common sense into good sense is often hurried by the claims of logic and method to inaugurate a republic of knowledge. Language suffers in all this because clarity is the enemy of ornament and epiphany, and throws out poetry in favor of public knowledge, health, and security.

Method is hostile to the gratuities of poetry and myth. Thus science seeks to conscript sociology to its ideals of well-ordered speech. Sociology in turn is tempted to regard the efficiency of speech as the workings of an external order of progressive revelation moving from magic and myth to science and plain sense. Moreover, sociology is enamored with mastery and technique. But these are equally the responses of speech in addressing nature, language, and society as the others of dialogue.

The acquisition of sociological speech does not begin with the postulate of social facts. In Durkheim and Weber the birth of sociology owes as much to prayer—society is God, society is spirit—as to the method of its fathers. In this, sociology is tied to singing itself as much as the world it furnishes. Where would sociology find any other path to knowledge than science, and how would this shape its speech? It is not even possible to raise this question so long as sociology clings to the skirts of science without any knowledge of the place of science itself in the conversation of mankind. Rather, sociology must learn, as King Lear learned, that it is in ourselves that we encounter the division of reason working irresistibly against the kingdom of love, mutilating the power of language in its prayers, its names, and its truth-telling. Sociology must learn that in the end it is we who gather the world and are its true metamorphosis. For even in our asylums God's spies gather up the heavens against the day when they will prevent the Machiavellians and charlatans who twist the grain of our humanity.

> No, no, no, no! Come, let's away to prison;
> We two alone will sing like birds i'th'cage:
> When thou dost ask me blessing, I'll kneel down,
> And ask of thee forgiveness: so we'll live,
> And pray, and sing, and tell old tales, and laugh
> At gilded butterflies, and hear poor rogues
> Talk of court news; and we'll talk with them too,
> Who loses and who wins; who's in, who's out;
> And take upon's the mystery of things,
> As if we were God's spies: and we'll wear out,
> In a wall'd prison, packs and sects of great ones
> That ebb and flow by the moon.[4]

King Lear's lesson is the lesson of wild sociology. For what he has to learn against the demands of Hobbesian will and utility is the regeneration of the bonds of service and family, of the generics of natural society. Lear's tragedy is the tragedy of relation to which we are born, on which we depend for love, friendship, truth, and service. In youth we challenge relation; in old age we depend upon it for our peace. In all else we define it, defend it, resist it even to honor or destroy it. Relation is the metaphysics of our humanity; it is our alliance with the world's fools.

Sociological knowledge is a knowledge of metamorphosis. For it is we who are the substance and form of social life whose structure is in turn commentary upon its methodology and matter. "One cannot come back too often to the question what is

4. **King Lear**, Act V, Scene III.

knowledge and to the answer knowledge is what one knows."[5] It is in this sense that Harold Garfinkel has revealed to us the poetics of sociological knowledge in the everyday metamorphosis and method of its narrative. It is from this fundamental principle that wild sociology, or what Garfinkel calls "ethnomethodology," invokes a version of sociological knowledge that is neither narcissistic nor alien with regard to the intrinsic generosity of the platitudes of commonsense values and knowledge of the social world. "For Kant the moral order 'within' was an awesome mystery; for sociologists the moral order 'without' is a technical mystery. From the point of view of sociological theory the moral order consists of the rule-governed activities of everyday life. A society's members encounter and know the moral order as perceivedly normal courses of action—familiar scenes of everyday affairs, the world of daily life known in common with others and with others taken for granted."[6]

The conversable attitude of daily life is grounded in the monumental achievements of commonsense perception, knowledge, and values. These are the work of everyone and no one, furnishing the considerations and relevances of our living that lie upon us a daily and sacred part of the mind. For the most part rationalism in science and philosophy consists in the demand that things and action be conformable to the standards of rationality. Properly speaking, however, theory is only rational when it abides by the troublesome contingency of things and human conduct. The rationality of wild sociology, unlike scientific rationalism, refrains from imposing reason upon reality: it seeks rather to make sociological theory rational in the acceptance of the contingent modes of social reality. What Garfinkel calls the indexical or occasioned features of everyday talk and

5. Gertrude Stein, **Lectures in America** (Boston: Beacon Press, 1957), p. 11.
6. Harold Garfinkel, **Studies in Ethnomethodology** (Englewood Cliffs, N.J.: Prentice-Hall, 1967), p. 35.

conduct, namely, the very features of self-reference that scandalize the generality and abstraction of science, are precisely the scattering of our divinity in the mundane particulars of everyday living and its umbilical ties to the here-and-now practices of commonsense knowledge and values. All this keeps our talk to itself in the small gatherings of our lives, between families and among friends, in kitchens as in high places, protected only by the warmth of our own people and remembered kindly despite its pain and injuries.

> And thus, too, these families, not otherwise than with every family in the earth, how each, apart, how inconceivably lonely, sorrowful, and remote! Not one other on earth, nor in any dream, that can care so much what comes to them, so that even as they sit at the lamp and eat their supper, the joke they are laughing at could not be so funny to anyone else; and the littlest child who stands on the bench solemnly, with food glittering all over his cheeks in the lamplight, this littlest child I speak of is not there, he is of another family, and it is a different woman who wipes the food from his cheeks and takes his weight upon her thighs and against her body and who feeds him, and lets his weight slacken against her in his heavying sleep; and the man who puts another soaked cloth to the skin cancer on his shoulder; it is his wife who is looking on, and his child who lies sunken along the floor with his soft mouth broad open and his nakedness up like a rolling dog, asleep: and the people next up the road cannot care in the same way, not for any of it: for they are absorbed upon themselves: and the negroes down beyond the spring have drawn their shutters tight, the lamplight pulses like wounded honey through the seams into the soft night, and there is laughter: but nobody else cares. All over the whole round earth and in the settlements, the towns, and the great iron stones of cities, people are drawn inward within their little shells of rooms, and are to be seen in their wondrous and pitiful actions through the surfaces of their lighted windows by thousands, by millions, little golden aquariums, in chairs, reading, setting tables, sewing, playing cards, not talking, talking, laughing inaudibly, mixing drinks, at radio dials, eating, in shirt-sleeves, carefully dressed, courting, teasing, loving, seducing, undressing, leaving the room empty in its empty light, alone and writing a letter urgently, in couples married, in separate chairs, in family parties,

> in gay parties, preparing for bed, preparing for sleep: and none can care, beyond that room; and none can be cared for, by any beyond that room: and it is small wonder they are drawn together so cowardly close, and small wonder in what dry agony of despair a mother may fasten her talons and her vampire mouth upon the soul of her struggling son and drain him empty, light as a locust shell: and wonder only that an age that has borne its children and must lose and has lost them, and lost life, can bear further living; but so it is.[7]

Self is circumstantial through and through and is utterly lost if it does not learn to save circumstance in the expression of its needs and knowing. Wild sociology cannot trick the relation between self and circumstance by making of self or of circumstance a thing, an organization, or a contract. The corporeal composition of self and circumstance involves us in a daily metaphysics of contingency, relation, caprice, and corruption in which culture is not an abstract and universal organ but a concrete and circumstantial practice without any other resort than the great natural orders of our daily living.[8] Wild sociology embraces the common dilemma of making sense together that it must share with all other lay practitioners of the art. It exercises a limited reflexivity[9] that attaches us to the conversable particulars of use, limit, and value, which engender the immense perspectives of the world, of family, class, gender, truth, and rationality. Wild sociology refrains from the ecstasy of conventional sociology in the presence of hieratic values rather to celebrate the integrity of everyday conduct and its own artful accomplishment of concrete destinies. It is to be expected that such a sociology of everyday life will involve a certain outrage

7. James Agee and Walker Evans, **Let Us Now Praise Famous Men** (New York: Ballantine Books, 1966), pp. 51–52.

8. John O'Neill, "On Simmel's 'Sociological Apriorities,' " in **Phenomenological Sociology: Issues and Applications,** ed. George Psathas (New York: John Wiley & Sons, 1973), pp. 91–106.

9. John O'Neill, "Can Phenomenology be Critical?" **Philosophy of the Social Sciences** 2, no. 1 (March 1972): 1–13.

as well as systematic misunderstanding when viewed from the perspective of establishment sociology. There is a certain irony in the terms of this antagonism, for it is precisely wild sociology that is a sociology of convention and establishment because of its patient apprenticeship to the anonymous labor of social institution and of the great natural orders of our communal life.

In practice wild sociology achieves a return to things that is the direction of poetry. All of modern thought addresses nature's body, bringing reason to its sense through the recollection of the primacy of perceptual knowledge. In speaking of the poetics of everyday thought and emotion, I have in mind the connections between the seemingly hopeless condition of circumstance—the condition of no one in particular and yet of everyone—and the massive presumptions and uses of order in our sentimental and political lives. Moreover, this poetry is in keeping with the viewpoint of modern science, provided that in both cases we properly understand that the very notion of viewpoint in no way involves a fall into subjectivism and relativism. This needs to be said for the sake not only of critics but also of many who believe they are the new poets of relativity.

We deal in knowledge, perception, and values that are neither the universal acquisition of a disembodied and unsituated ego nor merely a local and willful imposition of sensory limits. Rather, the fact that the world has a different face for a fifth-century Athenian and a twentieth-century Torontonian, so far from making objective knowledge impossible, is the very organizing element of truth and its historical acquisition. Truth is never the achievement of once and for all agreements, any more than it is merely a temporary pact. These simple alternatives leave out of account the strength and appeal of local arrangements whose fame spreads upon the stream of generations, linking neighbors and posterity in the general labor of culture. "Culture for the dark-eyed men who meditate, argue, sing, preach, and dream in Ionia, Attica, Sicily, and Magna Graecia, means what is firm as opposed to what is unstable, what is fixed as opposed to what is fleeting, what is clear as opposed to what is obscure. Culture is not the whole of life, but only the moment of security, of certainty, of clarity. And the Greeks invent the concept as an instrument, not for replacing the spontaneity of life, but for making it secure."[10]

Today, of course, we are not much given to the patience of circumstance. We are sophisticated relativists, anthropologists, vulgar Freudians and Marxists, forever seeing through the candor of primitive use, weighing motive in the scales of class injustice, invoking that universal truth that is the trick of university, newspaper, and tourist culture. Modern culture assumes relativism so strongly that it will seem prescientific to deny it. We may grant this relativism and yet still reject its conclusion. For the relativity of science is a conclusion of classical mechanics rather than the sense of Einstein's relativity theory. Galileo and Newton regarded our empirical judgments of time, space, and motion as relative because they themselves postulated observer's absolute space, time, and movement. Einstein's mechanics rejects the absolutism of Euclidean space with the result that the relativity of space-time observations no longer yields mere appearances but a relative reality that is absolute because it is all we can know. The new relativity differs in its absolutism from that of the rationalist mechanics of Galileo and Newton inasmuch as it treats perspective as a constituent feature of reality. Thus viewpoint is an absolute ingredient of modern science and not at all a prescientific provincialism.

Yet in the social sciences we continue to treat knowledge as the conclusion of an absolute observer who confounds subjective experience in the relativity of appearance and perspective. In this way, the social sciences alienate the daily labor of each

10. José Ortega y Gasset, **Meditations on Quixote,** trans. Evelyn Rugg and Diego Marin (New York: W. W. Norton & Co., 1961), p. 96.

one of us in bringing to bear our viewpoints, beliefs, attitudes, needs, and desires into the great stock and exchange of human culture and its shaping sensibility. **We are ourselves and our circumstances:** this is the natural light of a wild sociology that has genuinely absorbed the convergence of science and poetry in the modern world.[11] It is from our circumstance that things and others have the ancestral shape of need, of friend and family, of instrument and advice. It is from circumstance that we have our moods like the changing light of day, our resignation, our hope, and our brooding memory. We and our circumstances are the material of metaphor and relevance as well as of plain talk, vice, and unfulfilled virtue. And we are these things day in and day out, and what we are in the midst of these things, small towns, trades, and landscapes, is their very light and our own reflection, their own offering and our own gift. The panorama of our beliefs, needs, and values is not given to the unsituated perspective of science; it is an everyday reality forged from the conversable uses and sufficiencies of our daily living.

> . . . Are we perhaps here only to say: house,
> bridge, brook, gate, jug, olive tree, window,—
> at best: pillar, tower . . . but to **say** them, understand me,
> **so** to say them as the things within themselves never
> thought to be. Is not the hidden craft
> of this secretive earth when she urges two lovers on,
> that in their feelings each and everything should be
> transported?
> Threshold: what is it for two

11. "I am myself plus my circumstance, and if I do not save it, I cannot save myself. **Benefac loco illi quo natus es,** as we read in the Bible. And in the Platonic school the task of all culture is given as 'to save the appearances,' the phenomena, that is to say, to look for the meaning of what surrounds us" (Ortega y Gasset, **Meditations on Quixote,** pp. 45–46). Cf. Julian Marias, **José Ortega y Gasset: Circumstance and Vocation,** trans. Frances M. Lòpez-Morillas (Norman, University of Oklahoma Press, 1970); and Owen Barfield, **Saving the Appearances: A Study in Idolatry** (New York: Harcourt, Brace & World, Harbinger Books, 1965).

lovers that they wear down a little
the older threshold of their own door. They too, after
the many before them, and before all those to come . . . ,
lightly.

Here is the time for what can be **told,** here its home.
Speak and confess. More than ever
do the things we live with fall away, and
what displaces them is an act without image.
An act under crusts it will rip as soon
as its strength outgrows them and seeks new limits.
Between the hammer strokes
our heart endures, as does
the tongue between the teeth, which still
is able to praise.

Praise to the Angel our world, not the untellable:
you can't impress **him** with grand emotion. In the cosmos
where he so powerfully feels, you're only a newcomer.
Then show him some simple thing, grown up through
generations
till it became ours, and lives near our hands and in our eyes.
Tell him of things and he'll stand astonished, as you stood
beside the rope-maker in Rome, or with the Nile potter.
Show him how joyful a thing can be, how innocent and ours,
how even lamenting sorrow can take purely its own form,
serve as a thing, or die in a thing—and in ecstasy
escape beyond the violin. And these things,
that live only in passing, understand that you praise them;
fugitive, they look to us, the most fugitive, for rescue.
They want us entirely to transform them in our invisible
hearts
into—oh, infinitely—into us! Whoever we finally are.[12]

Wild sociology is a species of intellectual love. For sociology cannot turn away from the consenting goods of human need and natural circumstance that bind us to the perfection of things as our own accomplishment and as the salvation of our souls. Sociology truly seeks a radical comprehension of human circumstance. But it has vulgarized its vocation in an impatient

12. Rainer Maria Rilke, **The Duino Elegies,** trans. Stephen Garmey and Jay Wilson (New York: Harper & Row, 1972), The Ninth Elegy, pp. 66–67.

reduction of circumstance to environment, organization, class, and ethnicity. Sociology has reduced circumstance through its mathematical collection of motive as self, thing, and environment to nothing else than sociology's own possibilities of world-making.[13] To the extent that it is successful in this enterprise, sociology is an alien science and a hostile medium rather than the beneficent shell of human circumstance and need.

In its attachment to circumstance, wild sociology saves the appearances of communal life from the normative ironies of the scientific attitude that abstracts from the horizonal truths and inscapes of daily living. Circumstance is not the instrument of reason, nor is it its bare material waiting upon the inspiration of science for its furnishing and interpretation. Circumstance is the inscape of sense and reason. It is the self's surround, the open sublation of inside and outside, of self and thing, of self and other. Circumstance is the reminiscence of sensibility and reason folding back upon the world's embrace of our daily living. Human circumstance is never a bare instrument but rather a loving care and inscription of those fantastic universals that are the poetry of time's body and Vico's first conception of wild sociology.

13. I intend to treat the mathematical and nonmathematical collection of thought, self, thing, and speech in my forthcoming **On the Way to Sociology,** first presented as lectures to the Department of Psychology, Duquesne University, Pittsburgh; the Department of Sociology and the Program in Modern Thought and Literature, Stanford University; and the School of Social Science, University of California at Irvine, in January and February, 1973. Here and in this later work I am happy to acknowledge the thoughts of my colleague Alan Blum, in **Theorizing** (London: Heinemann Educational Books, 1974). I want also to thank Hans Mohr, Kurt Wolff, Hans Bremer, and Ken Morrison for helping me to improve my first attempts at this work.

3 Time's Body

Ours is an age in which everything is said clearly and concisely. What is not clear and concise only points to the need to keep up with this age. The clarity of our age is not an easy acquisition, though its style and uses are to be presumed upon among enlightened men held responsible to the larger circle of those who place their faith in clarity as the fruit and sustenance of the republic of science and democracy.

Clarity in language and thought naturally allies itself with frank and open conduct. Thus we are unwilling to allow privacy to our public men; and since no one wishes to be accused of private ways, every man seeks to conduct as much of his life in public as society can conveniently cater. If obscenity and pornography are issues in our age, as indeed they are, it is only because we wish everything to be seen in the light of day, without benefit of difference, without magic, and without any

I am grateful to Dr. Giorgio Tagliacozzo for the original invitation to consider Vico's philology in an essay for his **Giambattista Vico's Science of Humanity** (Baltimore: Johns Hopkins University Press, forthcoming), in which this chapter will also appear.

appeal to poetry. Thus we are as much concerned to exhibit corruption in the body politic as we are fixed upon celebrating the conquest of body odors. For cleanliness is next to clarity.

Our age reckons that language is the instrument of thought and that we have nothing to find in language that we have not ourselves put into it. Thus the well-formed languages of logic and science are calculated to separate language from the history of man's speech about himself in order to make of the future a thing of rule. Language itself encourages our ambition to rule the world as a thing. For in its ordinary use language never obtrudes between us and the world, its virtue as the vehicle of thought and action being to efface itself. Thus it appears that we owe nothing to language except its proper use, which is ruled by the world's connections and not by anything our own life lends to language.[1] Clarity is therefore the only embellishment of scientific language that cultivates simplicity and precision in order to make of itself a universal prose.

The modern world holds time in its hand. We consider that we have broken with the past and that we are headed toward the future launched upon nothing else than our present abilities. This is a story that is related to us by our historians and social scientists in the unvarnished prose that is the emblem of their extroverted character. For we mean to make an open book of society and nature. It is essential to the success of this enterprise that we rid man and society of any universals other than those of science. Thus science is forgetful of the roots of its own practice and possibility and has no desire to be reminded of the sources of inspiration and madness that have brought history to the self-made arts of science, technology, and democracy.

It is a paradox of the age of prose that men are learning again

1. Maurice Merleau-Ponty, **The Prose of the World,** ed. Claude Lefort, trans. John O'Neill (Evanston, Ill.: Northwestern University Press, 1973).

to see and to hear, to read and to write, are learning to talk and to listen. This is especially disturbing in a society that has made an industry of knowledge and so presumes upon its expansion that communication hardly means more than the speed with which the republic of science and commerce consumes its own self-image. For communication is the soul of extroversion; it feeds off the dead body of language and the extinction of style. Yet amidst the ruins of language and the collapse of history and character, men begin to turn over words in search of oracles, of the myths and metaphors that restore the human family and the fantastic universals of time's body.[2]

Science means to set men free from the idols of everyday language and from the mysteries of arcane speech. To achieve its purposes scientific enlightenment must teach men to speak of history as progress and to conceive of society as the engine of character and motive. It is essential to this view that social facts are what they are only by means of clear and distinct rules of analysis and combination and that social facts are not in any way beholden to their profound interior or to their generic bonds. Thus sociological knowledge accumulates at the same time as men lose their collective memory. In this situation time's body fractures into the elements of individualism, contract, guilt, and violence. These are the material of history's progress and the daytime efforts of reason to reduce itself to an instrument without a body—a thinking calculus.

Enlightenment declares mankind to be a task of reason separated from passion and its own origins. Liberal history schedules reason in favor of the late born, unshackled by myth, family, and the body's dreams. Liberal enlightenment rules the world by making children out of three quarters of mankind; the other quarter learns to repress its origins in order to make civilization the engine of its discontent. Thus reason's war against

2. Norman O. Brown, **Closing Time** (New York: Random House, 1973).

oracles joins in the war against the body's orifices, which are the way in and the way out of the world's round.[3]

The modern world retains its youth while all else dies young or comes to unwanted old age. Science, technology, and democracy are unseasonable work inspired by change and progress wrought upon language, reason, and the passions in order to make a thing of mankind without any regard for the great body of human time. Socrates turned from the study of science in order to live among men, to dwell upon the life that is gathered in men's language and with a chance of wisdom risked in irony, to prepare for death. For Socrates understood, just as Vico was to argue later, that science is a passion of youth but quite unable to make men.

> And to his cost he learned that that study [geometry] proper to minute wits is not easy for minds already made universal by metaphysics. So he gave up this study as one which chained and confined his mind, now accustomed through long study of metaphysics to move freely in the infinite of genera; and in the constant reading of orators, historians and poets his intellect took increasing delight in observing between remotest matters ties that bound them together in some common relation. It is these ties that are the beautiful ornaments of eloquence which make subtleties delightful.[4]

Science makes the world over in the name of men unconcerned with self-ignorance; it hopes to measure wisdom by what a man knows about the world outside and beyond his own life. Thus science is always defeated by death, or rather, science ignores death because it presumes upon the future to accomplish its task. But Socrates understood that knowledge is redeemed only by death and community and in the gathering of men according to their own manner of speaking and living.

3. Norman O. Brown, **Love's Body** (New York: Random House, Vintage Books, 1968).

4. **The Autobiography of Giambattista Vico,** trans. Max Harold Fisch and Thomas Goddard Bergin (Ithaca, N.Y.: Great Seal Books, 1963), p.123.

Thus Socratic ignorance anchors upon time's body and the human family whose conventions are the ground of man's nature. Socrates founds the tradition of vulgar metaphysics from which Vico later creates his wild sociology.

Kinship is the substance of wild sociology because Vico, like Socrates, understood that the good of knowledge lies in the world between men; in other words, in human institutions and not in the world outside of men, or in nature, except as science itself is a human institution. Philology is the method of Vico's new sociology because the acquistion of language is the same thing as our humanity, the same in our childhood as among other men whose ways we learn by understanding their language. For we are just as strange to ourselves as other men in other times are to us unless we learn the history of our language. Vico's wild sociology is therefore grounded in the love of language and kinship, in a poetry of the archetypes and fantastic universals that have shaped time's body into the natural institutions of human intellect and imagination.

> This was the order of human institutions: first the forts, after that the huts, then the villages, next the cities, and finally the academies.
>
> This axiom is a great principle of etymology, for this sequence of human institutions sets the pattern for the histories of words in the various native languages. Thus we observe in the Latin language that almost the whole corpus of its words had sylvan or rustic origins. For example, **lex**. First it must have meant a collection of acorns. Thence we believe is derived **ilex**, as it were **illex**, the oak (as certainly **aquilex** means collector of waters); for the oak produces the acorns by which the swine are drawn together. **Lex** was next a collection of vegetables, from which the latter were called **legumina**. Later on, at a time when vulgar letters had not yet been invented for writing down the laws, **lex** by a necessity of civil nature must have meant a collection of citizens, or the public parliament; so that the presence of the people was the **lex**, or "law," that solemnized the wills that were made **calatis comitiis**, in the presence of the assem-

bled **comitia.** Finally, collecting letters, and making, as it were, a sheaf of them for each word, was called **legere,** reading.[5]

The cycle of language is the cycle of our great family history. But enlightenment seeks to dissolve the human family into a political contract grounded in fraternal guilt. In this way imagination is cut off from its universal roots. Men are forced to abandon poetry in favor of that prose that is suited to speak about what men see who no longer see into themselves. The language of imagination is therefore pushed into dreams, myths, and poetry, which store up man's common nature as a treasure to be discovered only by those who still love words, language, and song. But Vico's wild sociologists are **philologists,** that is to say, men whose love of language loves mankind from its birth.

> It [the New Science] must begin where its subject matter began, as we said in the Axioms. We must therefore go back with the philologians and fetch it from the stones of Deucalion and Pyrrha, from the rocks of Amphion, from the men who sprang from the furrows of Cadmus or the hard oak of Vergil. With the philosophers we must fetch it from the frogs of Epicurus, from the cicadas of Hobbes, from the simpletons of Grotius; from the men cast into this world without care or aid of God, of whom Pufendorf speaks, as clumsy and wild as the giants called "Big Feet," who are said to be found near the Strait of Magellan; which is as much to say from the cyclopes of Homer, in whom Plato recognizes the first fathers in the state of the families.[6]

Modern man lives as unsure of birth, marriage, and death as he does of the past and the future. This is strange because modernity is essentially a historical consciousness, obsessed with the stages of its own development. But liberal individual-

5. **The New Science of Giambattista Vico,** trans. from the 3d ed. (1744) by Thomas Goddard Bergin and Max Harold Fisch, revised and abridged (Ithaca, N.Y., and London: Cornell University Press, 1970), p. 36.
6. Ibid., p. 57.

ism cannot achieve more than a guilty love of the past, for the past is beholden to its family gods who rule the beginning and end of human life, determining its fruits and sorrows. Modern man aspires to live outside of the family; his need is to make of birth and death mere null points in order to destroy time's body. Thus modern society submits equally the womb and the grave to its cosmetic denials. The present, then, is only the dream place of beautiful losers.

Language fractures in the modern world because our speech is no longer the reflection of anything that is ordered either inside or outside of us. Every historical order ultimately collapses the literary, artistic, and philosophical languages that for a time allowed an age to speak of itself and to gather its particular goods and evils. It is an axiom of Vico's wild sociology that if history is at all saved it is saved by language. For it is in the history of our language that we recover our humanity. It is in language that we discover the gradual making of the institutions that have made us human.

But then the wild sociologist is required against the spirit of the times to love the human family and to make a method out of remembrance and imagination. The wild sociologist will therefore need to avoid telling mankind's story according to the pattern of progress, as though man had a future quite beyond himself or unweighted by his past. Yet to reject this story requires more strength than was needed by the early heroes, for it requires looking back into the face of the family and to our first awkward steps toward humanity. Thus it is easier to reject the gods than to reject man but harder still to accept man. Such is the piety of wild sociology.

Vico's conception of wild sociology is patient with its own origins and thus it does not speak solely through the mouths of gods and heroes. By the same token, it is not anxious about ends and so it does not hasten man's speech with logic and science. The pillars of the poetic commonwealth are religion, marriage, and burial, which found our humanity upon what men everywhere owe to themselves and not to priests, philosophers, or scientists. For human law is nothing but the bonds men place upon themselves to clothe their nudity in the civil beauty of family, community, and speech.

Man is nothing else than the way he talks about himself. Wild sociology holds together the fractured speech of modernity because it rejoins time to its body, to its seasons and cycles of human fortune.[7] It is an axiom of wild sociology that science never leaves man behind; science itself is one more faith of mankind, another version of family and deliverance. This is a necessary axiom, since we should otherwise have no call to read Vico himself anymore than he had to read others before him. The call that is answered in Vico is the same call that language makes upon us today. It is the call for the renewal of the springs of language dried out in an age of precision and clarity.

> But the nature of our civilized minds is so detached from the senses, even in the vulgar, by abstractions corresponding to all the abstract terms our languages abound in, and so refined by the art of writing, and as it were spiritualized by the use of numbers, because even the vulgar know how to count and reckon, that it is naturally beyond our power to form the vast image of this mistress called "Sympathetic Nature." Men shape the phrase with their lips but have nothing in their minds; for what they have in mind is falsehood, which is nothing; and their imagination no longer avails to form a vast false image. It is equally beyond our power to enter into the vast imagination of those first men, whose minds were not in the least abstract, refined, or spiritualized, because they were entirely immersed in the senses, buffeted by the passions, buried in the body. That is why we said above that we can scarcely understand, still less imagine, how those first men thought who founded gentile humanity.[8]

7. Stuart Hampshire, "Joyce and Vico: The Middle Way," **The New York Review of Books** 20, no. 16 (October 18, 1973).
8. **The New Science of Giambattista Vico**, p. 76.

We read Vico today because our task is to renew the names of things together with the edges of their special silence. Vico recalls that benign nominalism that brought men out of the forests into the light of language. At first men were the children of time's body; they sang out the names of things in bodily play, in pleasure and love. They built up language through metaphor, that is, by playing upon words. And because they were not ashamed of their bodies they named things after the body and gave to nature the body's own moods and sensual speech.

> The human mind is naturally inclined by the senses to see itself extremely in the body, and only with great difficulty does it come to understand itself by means of reflection.
>
> This axiom gives us the universal principle of etymology in all languages: words are carried over from bodies and from the properties of bodies to signify the institutions of the mind and spirit.[9]

Today we recall our ancestral condition not because we mean to be ruled by it but because we cannot be sure of our future without trying to hold together how man began. Vico's wild sociology saves reason by anchoring it to time's body and its civil beauty. For reason is not the zero point of passion but rather an involvement in the needs of our time acquired through a language that inhabits us and through which we in turn make our lives. The life of reason is therefore inseparable from its beginnings in poetry, myth, religion, and vulgar metaphysics. Reason is human when it is not forgetful of these origins but rather remembers them kindly for the sake of its own birth.

> The most sublime labor of poetry is to give sense and passion to insensate things; and it is characteristic of children to take

9. Ibid., p. 36.

inanimate things in their hands and talk to them in play as if they were living persons.

This philologico-philosophical axiom proves to us that in the world's childhood men were by nature sublime poets.[10]

Vico inspires us with our own language just as he renewed in himself Latin eloquence. Thus etymology is the music of Vico's wild sociology inviting us to hear our beginnings in the birth of language. Therefore, thinking is not ahead of speaking and speaking is not ahead of our bodies, so that thinking is not ahead of time's body, which is the time our senses need to become human, to speak, and to think. In any man whose thinking listens to his speaking there is founded the soul's city, hearkening to the principles, nature, and laws of mankind. But to listen to principle and nature is to begin again, to remake sense and sensuousness, to make of time's body a renaissance of reason and its divine pleasure. This is a communal birth, and history is its only midwife, for the soul's deliverance is nowhere else than into this beautiful world.

Finally, beginning with the idea by which every slight slope was called **mundus** (whence the phrases **in mundo est, in proclivi est,** for "it is easy"; and later everything for the embellishment of a woman came to be called **mundus muliebris**), when they came to understand that the earth and the sky were spherical in form, and that from every point of the circumference there is a slope toward every other, and that the ocean bathes the land on every shore, and that the whole of things is adorned with countless varied and diverse sensible forms, the poets called this universe **mundus** as being that with which, by a beautifully sublime metaphor, nature adorns herself.[11]

Like birth itself the human world comes about only in a given time and place marked by our weakness as much as by our strength, by pain as much as joy, by ugliness as much as beauty.

10. Ibid. p. 29.
11. Ibid., p. 226.

But at no time is human nature, whether bestial or savage, heroic or divine, anything less than man's nature. This nature is not wholly passionate, for otherwise we should not have established any public grounds of truth nor any of the fixed institutions of society. Yet we ought not to attribute to men more of reason and calculation than governs the present age. For then we should make of society a preposterous contract, or else a noble lie, instead of a family that has gathered despite what it has reasoned for itself, despite its lusts and its powers.

Vico's wild sociology is a science of reason renewed. Although it is born in the age of men, wild sociology gathers its own beginnings poetically from the temples of the sky from which all human institutions and sciences are handed down. Vico's wild sociology collects its own rough origins, recalling what it owes to our domestic labors in gathering acorns and animals, binding men and letters in law and parliament.

Vico's wild sociology is ultimately a life science. He who undertakes its work must penetrate the veil of time that separates his thinking life from the brooding body that is the place of reason and sense and their sole monument. For man is a work of his own hands and eyes, of his own lips and ears, a drama of his own passion and his own reason. Thus the eloquence of science and the civil beauty of law and religion are the true embellishments of humanity.

4
Wild Sociology

Science always obliges us to forget what we know. In this way we learn much though we may still lack wisdom. In the case of the natural world, our power over things is compensation enough for the separations of knowledge. But in the social world we cannot start with any certain distance between what we know ordinarily and the reports of sociology. For the social world does not wait upon the constructions of scientific reasoning. It makes sense from the first day until the last in the all-day and everyday surroundings of others whose life we share. Nothing lies outside of this circumstance, neither its ignorance nor its fears, neither its joys nor its injuries. The mystery of this circumstance measures the poverty of sociology.

Wild sociology seeks to establish how it comes about that without any explicit appeal to rule or benefit of science, what we ordinarily know and value, and in the variety of ways that we come to know it, has the massive feature of being "known in common with others"—how, in other words, commonsense knowledge and values achieve the status of fact or, rather, **moral fact.** It is here that we adopt Garfinkel's recommendation that we treat the presuppositions of the natural attitude of daily life as maxims of everyday conduct through which we derive our average sense of competence and moral membership with the institutions and values that are our daily circumstance. In other words, wild sociology treats the natural attitude as an **ethnomethodology** in which, for example, questions and answers, time and place, work, self-revelation, and advice, are the ways we have of deciding the sensible and warrantable status of events or actions by referring to their particulars as occasional evidence of our institutions of family, home, school, manhood, sincerity, and true love. These are in turn the reasonable grounds of our talk and commitments and could never be wholly the work or accomplishment of the social sciences.

We ordinarily experience the everyday social world as something that has preceded us and now faces us as an orderly scheme of things whose interpretation is handed on to us by parents, teachers, and almost anyone with whom we live and learn. On the basis of the general legacy of language and knowledge into which we are born, we use and enjoy the world in typical ways; we sit in the shade of trees, avoid barking dogs, drink milk, eat the right things, and run to mother for protection. The way in which we speak and act in the world and among others is shaped by our immediate purposes and conventions, which furnish a schema of relevances regarding what features of the world are to be selected for generalization, rule of thumb, reminiscence, use, and avoidance. We commonly assume that things will continue to be as we have known them and that we can go about our business in a routine way . . . and so on . . . and so forth . . . so as to minimize doubt and decision. Or, when something goes wrong, we expect to be able to regularize it, to fix it without having to take apart the whole scheme of things on which we have relied so far.

In the natural attitude of our daily lives the world has for us certain and constant features. We assume that the objects, persons, and regions of the world with which we are familiar will continue to be as they are; similarly, we assume that the experiences and emotions we have relied upon hitherto will continue to work for us as before. We assume that the world is amenable to our purposes and needs and that we shall be able to realize our interests through action in and upon the world. Of course, each of these expectancies may fail to be realized, producing practical and emotional as well as theoretical problems. When this happens we do not entertain open and permanent doubts about our knowledge in general but only insofar as this enables us to restore what is questionable in our working knowledge, belief, and values.[1]

The world as we know it presents itself to us in a massive face, the faces of family and friends, of street and neighborhood, with receding contours of familiarity and reach that we expect to be able to penetrate without becoming entirely lost and without meeting others with totally incommunicable ways. Each of us has a certain amount of "expert knowledge" for his particular needs, or else available upon thorough inquiry and application. But the greater part of this knowledge will be merely what it is necessary to know for all practical purposes, as tricks of the trade, rules of thumb, proverbial and folk wisdom. Where our general knowledge suffices for the definition of our task and situation, that is to say, where it enables us to discover its theme and its elaboration in and by particulars of the situation so as to engage its normal values, likelihoods, and causal texture, then we are able to treat what is required of us as a routine matter. We may, of course, be frustrated in our expectations and activities. But any stoppage in our conduct is

1. Alfred Schutz, **Collected Papers**, vol. 3, **Studies in Phenomenological Philosophy**, ed. Ilse Schutz (The Hague: Martinus Nijhoff, 1966); Alfred Schutz, **Reflections on the Problems of Relevance**, ed. Richard M. Zaner (New Haven, Conn.: Yale University Press, 1970); José Ortega y Gasset, **Man and People**, trans. Willard R. Trask (New York: W. W. Norton & Co., 1957).

perceived in the frame of its overall temporal course, which allows for others to see what has gone wrong, give help where needed, and so get us on our way.

These commonsense presumptions of conduct are the basis, then, for our being open to the influence of others, to their advice and aid. It enables others to see what we are up to and where we are, and thus to sustain a common schema of here-and-now, here-and-there relevances, that is to say, to locate the **occasional** or **indexical** properties[2] of the other person's action or talk and thus to generalize its sense. Thus in the commonsense attitude our own presence in the world is regarded as directly relevant to our understanding of the world and others and in turn their understanding of us. For example, what I am saying now depends very much on how I have approached this work, on how I try to breathe into it the sense to be made of it by us together once you share in it as a reader and as one who can be called upon to have some general sense of the allusions, the references, and the overall question that I am addressing. I am aware, of course, that you will not see things exactly as I do, reading rather more or rather less into what I am saying than what I have in mind to say. By the same token, there is a chance that I am thinking along the very same lines as some of my readers, or that they are even ahead of me. But whatever the background differences among us, we assume as a matter of course, though not without art, that we can share viewpoints, sentiments, and beliefs without elaborate recourse to the disciplines of logic and science. This reasoning, however, is not established without general discussion, through which we always seek the resource of agreement.

2. Harold Garfinkel, **Studies in Ethnomethodology** (Englewood Cliffs, N.J.: Prentice-Hall, 1967), chap. 1, "What is Ethnomethodology?" pp.1–34; and Edmund Husserl, **The Crisis of European Sciences and Transcendental Phenomenology: An Introduction to Phenomenological Philosophy**, trans. David Carr, (Evanston, Ill.: Northwestern University Press, 1970), p. 122.

> In exactly the way that persons are members to organized affairs, they are engaged in serious and practical work of detecting, demonstrating, persuading through displays in the ordinary occasions of their interactions the appearances of consistent, coherent, clear, chosen, planful arrangements. In exactly the ways in which a setting is organized, it **consists** of methods whereby its members are provided with accounts of the setting as countable, storyable, proverbial, comparable, picturable, representable—i.e., accountable events.[3]

The commonsense attitude of everyday life is not just a given. It is something that is evinced in our social conduct as part of our claim to a grasp of how things are, as our ability to handle our social surroundings, relevant others, and our own face. The attitude of everyday life is thus not simply a cognitive attitude but also an expressive or ethical attitude, which Garfinkel refers to under the concept of **trust,** or "a person's compliance with the expectancies of the attitude of daily life as a morality."[4] It is a feature of everyday life that it supports our self-conceptions much of the time so that it is only when for some reason it leads us on to a disappointment or failure that we become aware of our self-investment in the way we see things. To withdraw such investments and to find new outlets for old selves can be painful indeed; it requires the presence of others, even of the very persons who may have led us on, as they may later confess.

We are naturally surprised and shocked when things do not conform to our commonsense expectations of them. Every question of fact raises questions of moral identity as well as cognitive competence. We assume there is a world held in common that has certain constitutive features of sharedness which we manage in a self-patterned way, working back and forth, glossing meaning, taking particulars as evidence of an

3. Garfinkel, **Studies in Ethnomethodology,** p. 34.

4. Harold Garfinkel, "A Concept of, and Experiment with 'Trust' as a Condition of Stable Concerted Actions," in **Motivation and Social Interaction,** ed. J. O. Harvey (New York: The Ronald Press Company, 1963), pp. 187–238.

order of events yet to be established and, in turn, using this emerging order of events as "evidence" of the sense of its particulars. We regard the working of this scheme of things not just as an essay in knowledge but rather the same thing as a moral claim to our grasp of reality, of our competence and responsibility in the working of an order of events to which we are partner, so that commonsense knowledge of social structures is for us the same thing as moral knowledge.

The scientist, it is said, breaks with the daily world of the natural attitude. He lays aside the common fabric of belief, habit, and custom in the service of a systematic doubt and his subscription to rationally constructed knowledge. In the pursuit of doubt the scientist aims at the overthrow of conventional knowledge, the destruction of routine, and the emancipation of choice and decision. To achieve this the scientist must disengage himself from the world of pragmatic interest and relevances and thereby reinterpret the world solely in keeping with his own scientific purposes, namely, to achieve the solution of a problem for its own sake.[5] Even with regard to his solution, the scientist is prepared to see it defeated, improved upon, or made more rigorous and free of contradiction. The scientist also suspends the spatiotemporal relevances motivated by his own presence in the world. He adopts a timeless and objective stance in which space-time coordinates function solely to state the conditions for repeating an experiment. Because the scientist has no "here" within the world and is immune to the reciprocity of viewpoint, with its horizons of intimacy and generality, he is obliged to construct a **model actor** to whom he

5. Max Weber, "Science as a Vocation," in **From Max Weber: Essays in Sociology**, trans. and ed., Hans Gerth and C. Wright Mills (New York: Oxford University Press, 1958) pp. 129–156. Cf. Herminio Martins, "The Kuhnian 'Revolution' and Its Implications for Sociology," in **Imagination and Precision in the Social Sciences**, ed. T. J. Nossiter, A. H. Hanson, and Stein Rokkan (London: Faber and Faber, 1972) pp. 13–58; Robert W. Friedrichs, **A Sociology of Sociology** (New York: The Free Press, 1970).

imputes a **rational consciousness** interacting with others destined similarly to act like any-rational-man.

> The homunculus is invested with a system of relevances originating in the scientific problem of his constructor and not in the particular biographically determined situation of an actor within the world. It is the scientist who defines what is to his puppet a Here and a There, what is within his reach, what is to him a We and a You or a They. The scientist determines the stock of knowledge his model has supposedly at hand. This stock of knowledge is not socially derived and, unless especially designed to be so, without reference to social approval. The relevance system pertinent to the scientific problem under scrutiny alone determines its intrinsic structure, namely, the elements "about" which the homunculus is supposed to have knowledge, those of which he has a mere knowledge of acquaintance and those others he just takes for granted. With this is determined what is supposed to be familiar and what anonymous to him and on what level the typification of the experiences of the world imputed to him takes place.[6]

Sociological accounts are beset by the pervasive problem of the encounter between the everyday world of the commonsense natural attitude and the problem-specific interests of scientific inquiry and explanation. There are a variety of ways to express this difficulty. The particular approach that I should like to develop starts from the problem of the **mutual accountability** of the commonsense and scientific attitudes. It is possible, for example, out of evolutionary and rationalist fervor, to dismiss the articulation of commonsense knowledge as an idol of the marketplace from which science delivers us. Such an attitude has the support of the philosophical tradition and serves to qualify the superior social status that men of knowledge claim for themselves by appealing to the asceticism of rational thought in its struggle with license and foolishness. But this tradition belies itself inasmuch as it also appeals to the

6. Alfred Schutz, **Collected Papers**, vol. 1, **The Problem of Social Reality**, ed. Maurice Natanson (The Hague: Martinus Nijhoff, 1964), pp. 41–42.

sobriety of common sense to rescue us from the intoxications of speculative thought. For what is reasonable in human affairs is often found to be closer to common sense than is flattering for the scientists of conduct. Men are ordinarily aware that they are born much like any other men into a world whose ways and wisdom precedes them. So far from inspiring subjectivity and disorder, common sense allies itself with that proper human folly that men find it necessary to acquire to live with themselves. True folly is alien to the corrosive fantasy of perfectly rational character and community.

It is in the interest of scientific sociology to destroy custom and to deride convention in order to make of human assembly a rule of reason. In this unseasonable aspiration sociology strives to be immune to the exigencies of conviviality and collective sentiment. If this were at all a possibility, then sociology would truly be a science of difference, that is, of egoism, interest, and violence collected in the division of labor, in contract, and in the republic of method. But it is precisely this aspiration that limits scientific sociology to the rule of appearances. This rule in turn saves the rational management of social life by hiding its antisocial foundations. It is in this fashion that Erving Goffman reveals to us the folly of descriptive social science. That is to say, his labor shows that there is nothing behind the surfaces of sociological description once sociology itself is no longer beholden to the grounds of collective life.[7] In such a situation sociological description merely glosses the practices of vanity, equal hope, and the fear of death. Once scientific sociology engages in the unseasonable folly of breaking with communal sense, its own appeal becomes problematic, or

7. Erving Goffman, **The Presentation of the Self in Everday Life** (Garden City, N.Y.: Doubleday & Co., Anchor Books, 1959); **Relations in Public: Microstudies of the Public Order** (New York: Harper & Row, Harper Colophon Books, 1973); Daniel C. Foss, "Self and the Revolt against Method", **Philosophy of the Social Sciences** 2, no. 4 (December 1972): 291–307.

rather, it is reduced to an uncertain voice crying against an uncommon society. For the assembly of society and sociology is not a power of science.

> But suppose, right here, some wise man who has dropped down from the sky should suddenly confront me and cry out that the person whom the world has accepted as a god and a master is not even a man, because he is driven sheeplike by his passions; that he is the lowest slave, because he willingly serves so many and such base masters. Or again, suppose the visitor should command some one mourning his father's death to laugh, because now his father has really begun to live—for in a sense our earthly life is but a kind of death. Suppose him to address another who is glorying in his ancestry, and to call him low and base-born because he is so far from virtue, the only true fount of nobility. Suppose him to speak of others in like vein. I ask you, what would he get by it, except to be considered by everyone as insane and raving? As nothing is more imprudent than unseasonable prudence. And he is unseasonable who does not accommodate himself to things as they are, who is "unwilling to follow the market," who does not keep in mind at least that rule of conviviality, "Either drink or get out"; who demands, in short, that the play should no longer be a play. The part of a truly prudent man, on the contrary, is (since we are mortal) not to aspire to wisdom beyond his station, and either, along with the rest of the crowd, pretend not to notice anything, or affably and companionably be deceived. But that, they tell us, is folly. Indeed, I shall not deny it; only let them, on their side, allow that it is also to play out the comedy of life.[8]

It belongs to scientific folly to reckon men more rational than they care to be. Such folly easily allies with political pride to make men the instruments of rational organization beyond their will. Sociology is soon conscripted to this task. Or rather, without self-knowledge sociology never comes to terms with the temptations of scientific folly. It is essential, therefore, that we investigate the nature of the conduct that is inquiry into the

8. Desiderius Erasmus, **The Praise of Folly,** trans. Hoyt Hopewell Hudson (Princeton, N.J.: Princeton University Press, 1941), pp. 37–38. Reprinted by permission of Princeton University Press.

lives of others. We must ask what it is—faith or method—that supports us in decentering our own life among others in order to make of it a dedicated focus of concern with the otherness of others. How do we accomplish this, what motivates its concern, how is it to be fulfilled? We are not to presume that it is the work of alienation: for it is not practiced outside of the umbilical ties between us and others who feed us, smile upon us, help, hurt, and puzzle us. Among men rationality is the incarnate pursuit of understanding that breeds in bodily presences. This is the sustaining bond of sociological inquiry. What would it mean to cut ourselves off from this union in order to make of sociology a science? If we could achieve such a distance, to what in the end should we apply sociology?

In the face of this question sociology attaches itself to scientific description. Yet in modern literature and science nothing is less certain than description. Or rather, there have been times and places where narrative was more of a settled attitude—or the very composition of a settled attitude. But today words come apart and leap from the sentences that try to hold them to literary conventions. Sense and nonsense are if anything rival sensibilities rather than the frame and limit of understanding. Thus nothing can be more passionate than the commitment to true social narrative, that is, to a narrative that is patient with the intimacies of ordered and disordered life, through which the body becomes flesh of the world and the world in turn is fleshed into the sense and nonsense of character and society.

Wild sociology acknowledges that it is born into the desperate circumstance of having to earn its living. For sociology is preceded by the marvelous acquisitions of commonsense living and pragmatic reasoning that make it impossible for sociology to begin, as does science, with a lack of confidence in man. Wild sociology has no other way than to assume its conventional debts to the great traditions of our senses, manners, and natural reason. Thus it has no other narrative allegiance than to the virtues and ways of daily living from which we build up the institutions of understanding and good will. Wild sociology cannot suspend the intimacies of need, of hope and injury, of tools and engines, of family and first love, nor of hate and broken friendship. These are never virtual engagements of ours attendant upon the commitments of speculative reason and its contracts of utility and profit. For our social life is not convertible to a thing of use, nor into an image of itself. Let this stand in the surrounds of abuse, utility, fantasy, machination, and contract that we bear, much as life holds against all its afflictions:

> The plainness and iterativeness of work must be one of the things which make it so extraordinarily difficult to write of. The plain details of a task once represented, a stern enough effort in itself, how is it possibly to be made clear enough that this same set of leverages has been undertaken by this woman in nearly every day of the eleven or the twenty-five years since her marriage, and will be persisted in in nearly every day to come in all the rest of her life; and that it is only one among the many processes of wearying effort which make the shape of each one of her living days; how is it to be calculated, the number of times she has done these things, the number of times she is still to do them; how conceivably in words is it to be given as it is in actuality, the accumulated weight of these actions upon her; and what this cumulation has made of her body; and what it has made of her mind and of her heart and of her being. And how is this to be made so real to you who read of it, that it will stand and stay in you as the deepest and most iron anguish and guilt of your existence that you are what you are, and that she is what she is, and that you cannot for one moment exchange places with her, nor by any such hope make expiation for what she has suffered at your hands, and for what you have gained at hers: but only by consuming all that is in you into the never relaxed determination that this shall be made different and shall be made right, and that of what is "right" some, enough to die for, is clear already, and the vast darkness of the rest has still, and far more passionately and more skeptically than ever before, to be questioned into, defended, and learned toward. There is no way of taking the heart and the intelligence by the hair and of wresting it to its feet, and of making it look this terrific thing in the eyes: which are such gentle eyes: . . . and they are to be

> multiplied, not losing the knowledge that each is a single, unrepeatable, holy individual, by the two billion human creatures who are alive upon the planet today; of whom a few hundred thousands are drawn into complications of specialized anguish, but of whom the huge swarm and majority are made and acted upon as she is: and of all these individuals, contemplate, try to encompass, the one annihilating chord.[9]

Repetition is the ground of character and true narrative and it is in our ways and it is what sociology needs to settle in our daily living. But sociology need not know what it needs to know, and that is what is difficult in the narrative it undertakes. For it may forsake its task in generalities, failing to call upon the names of the things that are its poetic sources. Sociology enlightens us with talk of individualism, equality, progress, and environmental improvement. But character and place each have roots that hold against what scientific sociology has in store for us. Sociology lets self go free, without place, or past, or any injury of family. Yet these things return upon us. Sociology, to save itself, treats them as "problems."

Wild sociology abides in the daily necessity of having every day to make of necessity a daily thing and not tomorrow's mother. We know this and what we know of it is that it is repetition, the daily repetition of our lives, which is in our lives every day and in our talk and in all our senses, that is the conversable ground of sociology's way. For this reason wild sociology hides its own name. It is neither outside nor above the holy places it seeks to enter. It has no commanding voice, for it shuns the prescriptions of method and the forced entries of science. Wild sociology seeks therefore to persuade and to charm; yet not irresponsibly, for it is faithful to the poetry and prayers of mankind. Method presumes upon its own practice and in this it is careless and indifferent toward the particulars

9. James Agee and Walker Evans, **Let Us Now Praise Famous Men** (New York: Ballantine Books, 1966), pp. 290–291.

that fall under its rule. Wild sociology rejects the rudeness of method that lacks any respect for the community that suffers its practices. By the same token, it is not simply conservative; rather it imposes upon its actions and speech the obligation to bring our lives together.

Wild sociology is beholden to its community. For the sociologist needs other men, just as men make a family out of their happiness and their sorrows and do not bear these alone. No man really seeks privilege and exception but as gifts to be shared in the celebration of family and community in remembering our victories and defeats, welcoming our arrivals, and mourning our departures. Such community is rarely granted to us and is not to be usurped by the privilege of science intolerant of the ways of welcome. Thus wild sociology defends the community it chooses to inhabit as the place of its deeds. In this it solicits the community's own reminiscence and powers of repetition, which furnish the commonplaces of its reflection and self-appraisal. In this way wild sociology is obliged to observe and to listen for the bottom nature of things, where they are not ruled by passivity but rather launched upon the resolution to bring life together in work, in speech, in faith, and in understanding. Wild sociology is therefore without any method of its own beyond this very celebration that counts upon the labors of others to bring together our thoughts and speech, to offer us a chance of love and understanding. Thus in making sense together we appeal to the world as flesh, as an omnipresence that is never the material of science, for it lacks distance and indifference upon our part.

> Many things then come out in the repeating that make a history of each one for any one who always listens to them. Many things come out of each one and as one listens to them listens to all the repeating in them, always this comes to be clear about them, the history of them of the bottom nature in them, the nature or natures mixed up in them to make the whole of

them anyway it mixes up in them. Sometime then there will be a history of every one.

When you come to feel the whole of anyone from the beginning to the ending, all the kind of repeating there is in them, the different ways at different times repeating comes out of them, all the kinds of things and mixtures in each one, anyone can see then by looking hard at any one living near them that a history of every one must be a long one. A history of any one must be a long one, slowly it comes out from them from their beginning to their ending, slowly you can see it in them the nature and the mixtures in them, slowly everything comes out from each one in the kind of repeating each one does in the different parts and kinds of living they have in them, slowly then the history of them comes out from them, slowly then any one who looks well at any one will have the history of the whole of that one. Slowly the history of each one comes out of each one. Sometime then there will be a history of every one. Mostly every history will be a long one. Slowly it comes out of each one, slowly any one who looks at them gets the history of each part of the living of any one in the history of the whole of each one that sometime there will be of every one.[10]

The physicalism of scientific observation and reflection, by which I mean the presumption of distance, seems to me to lead sociology into an imperialism of method and rationality that undermines the ritual wholeness of the daily particulars which constitute the fabric of individual integrity and communal endurance. Every individual and community stands to us as a monument of human possibility expressed in the faces, the hands, the music, the food, dwellings, and tools that men endure against the earth and the twistings of man's own arrangements. The cycle of these things is born in an expansion of hope and possibility that is gradually simplified toward death. It is the burden of wild sociology and its imaginative power to cultivate this cycle, to follow its seasons, its shaping and its bearings of life. Scientific sociology cannot be faithful to this task so long

10. Gertrude Stein, **The Making of Americans** (New York: Harcourt, Brace & Co., 1934), p. 128. Reprinted by permission of Harcourt Brace Jovanivich, Inc.

as it is the instrument of the willfulness within modern society to deny the cycle of life, to subvert its repetitions by externalizing them into mechanical organs of production and reproduction.

Sociology's pride lies in its method of scientific analysis and unification, the aim of which is to make of the world a thing of construction through and through. We should not accept without reflection the physics built into the very notion of reflection's distance. What is the distance between men? How should thinking stand outside of greetings, comings, and goings? In short, is not everything **between** men, is not everything nurtured in the fold of their **presence**? Sociology's face is toward the world though it does not love the world in its nature, its houses, its food and furniture, its music and dance, its prayers and its terrors. Sociology is outward-looking, for it seeks to reshape destinies in the mold of environment. It shrugs off the weight of birth and family, the connections of blood, and the inevitability of death, in favor of reform and revolution. Sociology is democratic and progressive. Its method is the future via men's souls. It espouses the contingencies of love in order to write freedom into the chances of birth, family, class, and neighborhood. Sociology is convinced that what is difficult in its task is corrigible through the efforts of education, science, and politics to reduce all human arrangements to matters of rule.

Wild sociology needs time, for it deals with surfaces beneath which there lies the silent, wild being that is our lives made from the legacy of this body and family of ours and from the work of our senses and intellect where they have touched others and taken from them some kind of knowing that can never be refused and must always venture itself again. Wild sociology is governed by a profound respect for the particulars of place, time, and conduct from which men build their associations and the institutions of trust that sustain their communal lives. Its narrative keeps faith with this trust through a self-conscious artfulness, in knowing that things are not as they are in order to facilitate a superficial realism or to indulge an idle aestheticism. These are species of contemplative thought that fail to attach us to the awesome work of particular and local deeds which are the connections of social life. For true sociological narrative is not the empty iteration of how things are, apart from how it is we know them to be as they are. That is to say, true narrative is the soul's conversation with its senses through which we are engaged in where we live and live as we know we do. This is the real ground of sociological description and inquiry, and thus wild sociology is irredeemably a folk art. To keep its word it requires of us a holy vigil.

5
The Holy Watch

Wild sociology opens in the reversal of the look, in the seer who is seen in that moment of prayer that joins us despite our daily trespasses. For the trespass of hands and eyes, of warmth and rejection, is the bread of our lives together. Sociological distance is not an empty space between us: it is the reach for what we have in common through our mundane needs and their natural orders of commerce and ritual. To stand outside of these ancestral bonds, as does the observer, is to risk home and loss of faith.

Sociology is the study of man. How strange! For how does man become an object of study? What are the motives for such a practice and how does it coexist with the forms of daily life that come under the optic of sociological observation? What is the faith that supports the sociologist in his life? How does he live with the conscience of seeing men other than how they see themselves? To whom does he attribute the folly of difference: to the vanity of those whom he observes or to the vanity of the community of rational men that guides his own comparisons? Such questions are likely to be regarded as mere rhetorical flourishes, as disingenuous attempts to arouse interest in the long-solved practicalities of sociological work. Worse still, they might restore apathy, inasmuch as the difficulty of sustaining the direction of the inquiry they raise convinces us of the strength of the old ways to which we inevitably return.

And yet there is something uncanny in the sociological vision. It is not to be entered into lightly, nor, once acquired, should it be allowed to harden so that the care for what we see is no longer embracing. We cannot assume that our ideological, political, professional, or aesthetic faith will always be lively to **the collective focus of seeing and being seen** that is the ground of social life. Indeed, our politics may harden the original openness through which our concern for others irrupted into our lives and determined us never again to live outside of the mutual regard that shapes our joys, our sorrows, and our hopes for every human undertaking, whether it is the building of a bridge or the birth of a child. Sociological vision is in reality more a structure of care and concern than any literal vision. It is the care that orders the wild commerce of our daily talk, lookings, helpings, hurts, and angers. By the same token, it is the display of our shared lives, of our own growth, and the place others have in our lives without which we should be diminished and lonely.

> It is becoming apparent that concern is a normal dimension of everybody, including scholars, and that for scholars in particular it is the corrective to detachment, and prevents detachment from degenerating into indifference. . . . It seems obvious that concern has nothing directly to do with the content of knowledge, but that it establishes the human context into which the knowledge fits, and to that extent informs it. The language of concern is the language of myth, the total vision of the human situation, human destiny, human aspirations and fears.[1]

1. Northrop Frye, "The Knowledge of Good and Evil," in **The Morality of Scholarship**, by Northrop Frye, Stuart Hampshire, and Conor Cruise O'Brien, ed. Max Black (Ithaca, N.Y., and London: Cornell University Press, 1967), p. 16.

Sociological concern is not averse to scientific method. Indeed, much of what is called the scientific attitude turns out to be a moral attitude that most of us practice in our daily lives. For few men act without a certain detachment and objectivity, and most are unwilling to fly in the face of contradiction and failure. In this regard, the social sciences are no weaker than the physical sciences because the concern that infects them is not at all a subjective impulse but rather a general respect of natures and mutual regard that is a large part of our civic culture. No one will deny that even in the arts the direction has been toward detachment and objectivity properly understood as human concern.[2] Thus the tendency in the arts and literature is to shape subjective concern in the objective labor of a **craft.**[3] And this is a necessary direction, despite the ruin of things and language, so long as men refuse to alienate the labor of culture and its representative sensibility. Sociological concern is not the easy expression of political demands or of immediate social reforms. These may equally express the fall of sociological concern into indifference, that is to say, into a neglect of the integrity of sociological concern and individual care. For there is a tension of responsibility in genuine sociological concern. This is ingrained in our double commitment to the value of the individual and to the value of the society that enhances and yet unavoidably obstructs these values.

The wild sociologist needs heart, ideas, and ideology. He needs faith in the tissue of human time and the weave of human place in which he is caught more subtly than any notion of community can convey. Conventionality is the pulse of his life, stretching back into times and over distances he no longer

2. Leo Steinberg, **Other Criteria: Confrontations with Twentieth-Century Art** (New York, Oxford University Press, 1972).

3. John O'Neill, **Sociology as a Skin Trade: Essays towards a Reflexive Sociology** (London: Heinemann; and New York: Harper & Row, 1972).

recollects, resisting the ravages of his method, recalcitrant to organization. Wild sociology labors on behalf of an infinity of mankind bonded against everything that threatens, distorts, cripples, and injures the human family. The concerns of scientific sociology are irredeemably tied to the daily institutions of politics, ideology, and professional practice. For this reason the language of sociology is at times an orchestration of human love and at times a distortion or a characterization of average values that stylizes sociological concern without any surrender to the particulars of its practice. Today more than ever, sociology is bewitched by its own language, its imperious generalizations, its ambitions of control, its usurpation of relevance. Sociology seduces us because its subject, like the pool of Narcissus, reflects the shadow of man even in its least concerns, while at its best it rejoices the connoisseurs of humanity in their comfortable and learned distance from its everyday hopes and injuries.

In **Let Us Now Praise Famous Men** James Agee introduces us to one of the deepest meditations upon the nature of wild sociology that I know, and I want now to follow the path that it opens for us. The immediate concern of Agee's work is a documentary study of three families engaged in tenant farming and picking cotton. However, from the very outset Agee is concerned to guard against the sentimental and ideological distortions of sociological concern that are so often invited by the topics of sociological investigation. At the same time, he is deeply conscious of the set of relationships, the fraternal bonds, he is about to weave between himself and his readers, between his concerned public and the subjects of his study—and most agonizingly of all, between himself and the families among whom he lives and whose lives he observes, very possibly to their harm or merely for the peculiar enjoyment of a chorus of humanitarian readers and do-gooders. Under the weight of these considerations Agee turns at times to the eye of the camera but also for the same reasons to the compassionate icon of crucified humanity. And this is the way of wild sociology.

The risk involved in sociological work is that it will service ideologies far removed from the particulars of human purpose or else be received as an art to service the vague humanitarian aesthetics of its consumers, its lay readers and middle-class students. In the first case, the ideological reception of sociological work hardly begins to fathom the depths of human injury and comes far too soon to conclusions regarding the tissue of human connections and the viruses of relation, contract, and organization. In the second, the aesthetic perception of sociological work is disembodied from the intersensory and ancestral connections of mankind, whose infinitude defies dissection into science or art to such an extent that any observation risks obscenity and distortion. Moreover, the very aesthetic sensibility for which such risks might be undertaken has an awesome public ability to absorb injustice, beauty, rage, horror, and frivolity.

Thus anyone who is tempted to succeed in appealing to such a monster as the public must ask himself what has become of his first wonder at the lives of those human beings whose innocence of such "twistings" was his opening to the mystery of collective life. There is a certain obscenity about watching any human being, standing outside of his life when really the only place to be is at his side, sharing the same life. We cannot all do the same work. We are born at different times and under different circumstances. Yet the basic human desire to be in roughly the same condition and way of life has over time been built up in the institutions of the law and the church, of the Enlightenment, and of the liberal and social democratic philosophies of equality, to an extent that even when we find ourselves in the most different circumstances we nevertheless feel that we share or are working toward a common humanity. There are a variety of ways of reinforcing this bond with our fellow man. We can do it by simply sending money to the African missions. We may join a left-wing or right-wing party, or become urban planners. All these activities are motivated by the assumption that we know what others need, want, and are all about. Yet in working on a common project or to produce a common humanity, we find ourselves engaged in different ways of life. We are as much cut off from one another through the division of labor involved in working together as we are brought together. We find ourselves living possibly more intense but certainly more and more narrow lives. It thus becomes all the more important to establish ideological, political, and moral bonds with our fellow man.

Sociology contributes to the cement of these relations. Indeed, it is part of a whole range of urban man's vicarious experience. The more we separate from rural settings and move into industrial settings, the more we re-create the rural as nostalgia, in folk song and folk art. Thus we are conscious that there are people out there on the farms, or down in the slums, or out in the colonies. And we persuade ourselves that we are not entirely cut off from these people because we read newspapers, watch television reports, and drink orange juice or coffee to keep them in jobs. Or else we rationalize our charitable sentiments in the hope that our money will find its way into every crack and cranny of needful society. When we listen to folk and country music, when we pick up a book about the Cuban revolution, or when we read about the mill hands in the nineteenth century, what makes this a reasonable thing to do is not just that we happen to be music fans or students of revolution or of economic history fans but that we believe there is a common humanity that is made over, preserved, and advanced through just such activities, through our concern with other ways of life and their bearing upon our own living.

Such humanitarian concerns would be impossible if we were to hold on to solipsistic conceptions of mind or if we were to separate the mind and the heart in our understanding of sociological care. The care and concern that establishes our social life is an **institution** of sentiment and science that is manifested as much in schoolchildren's gifts to the missions as in reading the pre-Socratic philosophers or manipulating Keynesian variables to stabilize the modern economy. Sociological work belongs to this pattern of civilized sentiment and knowledge. Nevertheless, we encounter a paradox of sociological concern, namely, that its own activity adds to the differences among men another alienation that is simultaneously the basis for its search for communality and care. This is not the simple observation that reflection presupposes leisure and is therefore ultimately tied to social exploitation. It is the existential predicament of the thinker, the artist, the priest, and the visionary that their otherworldliness is strange to the only world for which they have any care. They therefore have to instruct the world in the very things they have learned from the world. But if sociologists are at all successful in this, they acquire a style of life and appeal to an audience whose way of life in turn aggravates the injury and injustice suffered by our common humanity. Yet there is no escape from this commonplace. It is the bread of our fellow men and we cannot refuse it. The questions we raise about the reasons for sociological concern, about its rights and its motives, must be shared in the common talk of the sociologist or the artist and his public. Ultimately, these are questions of mutual trust to which we must lend ourselves as the sole means of discovering our own motives as well as the public response to them.

Agee asked himself whether his own sociological report was

anything more than the expression of the impotency he experienced when he went out to help some people whose lives he found much richer, much more mysterious, than his own, but whom he had supposed in some way to be simpler, more comprehensible, more subject to alteration, and thus to justify the reasons he had assumed to be his purpose as a writer or social reformer. Thus he is concerned with the possibilities of obscenity, voyeurism, and betrayal as the real motives of sociological work. If this is at all true, then he fears he himself is more misshapen than the people among whom he moves, "all thus left open and defenseless to a reverent and cold-laboring spy." A good part of what we call social science is the study of individuals who are miserable enough to be the object of sociological inquiry. The wealthy, for the most part, escape sociological investigation, or when they fail to, the reason is evidently the alien designs of Marxists and muckrakers. They are generally allowed to pass through life altogether before any inquiry is made about their way of life. Or else they are kind enough to leave us memoirs. But the poor and primitive do not write memoirs. Their lives have to be documented, which means that their lives are the subject of ethnographies, questionnaires, and films. Thus the practice of sociology is entirely dependent upon the different forms of access to other individuals' lives, at the same time that sociology pretends to be a remedy for such inequality.

But wild sociology is not merely a fascination with the lives of others. It is a kind of **vigil** we maintain as much in our talk and shared experience as in the look and watchful concern for our neighbors and their children. The vigilance I have in mind is not simply watching lest certain things happen. It is the vigil in which things are encouraged in their form, in which, so to speak, things and the people around us seem to grow in us and we in them. Such vigilance is not easily assumed, and it is for this reason that we see Agee struggling with the scruples of cameralike realism or else with the image of the Cross in his search for a redemptive mediation of the holy particulars of human life.

> For one who sets himself to look at all earnestly, at all in purpose toward truth, into the living eyes of a human life: what is it he there beholds that so freezes and abashes his ambitious heart? What is it, profound behind the outward windows of each one of you, beneath touch even of your own suspecting, drawing tightly back at bay against the backward wall and blackness of its prison cave, so that the eyes alone shine of their own angry glory, but the eyes of a trapped wild animal, or of a furious angel nailed to the ground by his wings, or however else one may faintly designate the human "soul," that which is angry, that which is wild, that which is untamable, that which is healthful and holy, that which is competent of all advantaging within hope of human dream, that which most marvelous and most precious to our knowledge and most extremely advanced upon futurity of all flowerings within the scope of creation is of all these the least destructible, the least corruptible, the most defenseless, the most easily and multitudinously wounded, frustrate, prisoned, and nailed into a cheating of itself; so situated in the universe that those three hours upon the cross are but a noble and too trivial an emblem how in each individual among most of the two billion now alive and in each successive instant of the existence of each existence not only human being but in him the tallest and most sanguine hope of godhead is in a billionate choiring and drone of pain of generations upon generations unceasingly crucified and is bringing forth crucifixions into their necessities and is each in the most casual of his life so measurelessly discredited, harmed, insulted, poisoned, cheated, as not all the wrath, compassion, intelligence, power of rectification in all the reach of the future shall in the least expiate or make one ounce more light: how, looking thus into your eyes and seeing thus, how each of you is a creature which has never in all time existed before and which shall never in all time exist again and which is not quite like any other and which has the grand stature and natural warmth of every other and whose existence is all measured upon a still mad and incurable time; how am I to speak of you as "tenant" "farmers," as "representatives" of your "class," as social integers in a criminal economy, or as individuals, fathers, wives, sons, daughters, and as my friends and as I "know" you? Granted—more, insisted upon—that it is in all

> these particularities that each of you is that which he is; that particularities, and matters ordinary and obvious, are exactly themselves beyond designation of words, are the members of your sum total most obligatory to human searching of perception: nevertheless to name these things and fail to yield their stature, meaning, power of hurt, seems impious, seems criminal, seems impudent, seems traitorous in the deepest: and to do less badly seems impossible: yet in withholdings of specification I could but betray you still worse.[4]

Sociological vigilance is the care of things in their wholeness and integrity. It is neither an averaging nor an irony. It is a way of seeing things round, of celebrating time and place and the endurance of their human bonds. The saving of particulars and the frail connections of the human family is work that rests upon a variety of faiths. It may be the work of the ideologist, the political reformer, the social planner. But these perspectives easily lose sight of the particulars of ordinary life. It is for this reason that the images of the camera and of the Crucifixion are the instruments of Agee's concern with the epiphany of human events. The problem is how to see the eye seeing and not the recorded eye: how to see the eye and how to listen to what we hear in the sounding of human care. This comes from our openness to the belonging together of our senses and the community of being that is the possibility we have of learning togetherness and watchfulness. There is an obvious sense in which we may be counted among the community of mankind. But our humanity is properly our orientation to the community of being as our destiny or allotment. This community, our nature, approaches us in the involvements of care, not as a lacking but as a presencing of our situation.

Care, then, is the domicile of our being together.[5] But our

4. James Agee and Walker Evans, **Let Us Now Praise Famous Men** (New York: Ballantine Books, 1966), pp. 91–92.

5. Martin Heidegger, **Essays in Metaphysics: Identity and Difference**, trans. Kurt F. Leidecker (New York: Philosophical Library, 1960).

being together is easily subject to sociological rule. The division of labor and technology that subordinates human identity and difference to the confrontation of man and nature represents the reduction of care to need and domination. Thus, despite the intricate calculations and exchanges involved in sociological rule, it proceeds by challenging the framework or **institution** of human concern and solicitude for our corporate membership.

Agee remarks, as we have already seen, that he is writing about human beings who are not in any way concerned with the problems of the artist, or the musician, or even the priest or social worker. The problems of writers, artists, priests and sociologists are entirely over the heads of the people. Those who have such concerns are strange beings. They are monsters of concern. They want to do good, they want to save, they want to express, they want to celebrate. They experience themselves as above or outside the lives of those for whom they care. Their efforts are infected with a kind of superfluity, with doubts concerning truth and reality that have no counterpart in the lives of those for whom they intend help. And further, if the sociologist or artist is at all successful in resolving his problem of concern and alienation, his work will be taken up by others in the reading public whose lives make their concern with it a matter of good taste, education, liberal consciousness, Christian concern, so that the writer's work becomes a double alienation of the original suffering and beauty or whatever it was he saw in the lives of his fellow men.

These problems surround Agee's approach to the subjects of his study. The Mass is the canopy of the approach, entrance, worship, and return to the world celebrated through its own offerings of the fruits of its labors. The Mass is therefore the natural framework of Agee's report. Nor is this a mere literary device. It is the resonance of the **Introibo,** which is the approach to the holy interior of another life with whom we communicate through the efficacy of the Crucifixion. We are not, of course, dealing here with matters of religious certainty. What is at stake is the openness of human life to the approach of the other whose need is irresistible, even though its intent or consequences may lie far beyond our understanding. The approach makes us aware that human life is huddled about its own purposes, in its belongings, its families, farms, towns, and villages. To enter a town or to approach someone is to encroach upon their welcome, to seek a kindness whose offer must bridge the first strangeness, the searching eyes, and the beginnings of talk that make the human bond.

Agee relates three encounters in which he approaches first a group of Negroes enjoying themselves, a white family, and then a young Negro couple out walking. In the first instance, Agee and Walker Evans are introduced to a Sunday morning family gathering of visitors and children all obliged to assemble and sing for the landlord's intruders. Agee is agonized by the privilege that forces an intrusion into the lives of these people who nevertheless maintain an inner calm and dignity despite the injury they feel at having to treat what is of absorbing concern to them as something that must give pride of place to the curiosity and indulgence of others.

> Meanwhile, and during all this singing, I had been sick in the knowledge that they felt they were here at our demand, mine and Walker's, and I could communicate nothing otherwise; and now, in a perversion of self-torture, I played my part through. I gave their leader fifty cents, trying at the same time, through my eyes, to communicate much more, and said I was sorry we had held them up and that I hoped they would not be late; and he thanked me for them in a dead voice, not looking me in the eye, and they went away, putting their white hats on their heads as they walked into the sunlight.[6]

On another occasion Agee and Evans come to a fork in the road where Agee asks directions from a family sitting on their

6. Agee and Evans, **Let Us Now Praise Famous Men**, p. 30.

porch—a young man, a young woman, their children, and an older man. The family is silent, all the while watching the approach of the two strangers. But it is not an empty silence that hangs between them. Agee and Evans are already caught in the conversation of eyes that sustains and marks their approach. Already much has been said between the silently knit family, drawn together by the daily necessity of preservation against the invasions of injustice, cruelty, and misunderstanding, and the chance relief of these in good times and by occasional kindnesses.

> None of them relieved me for an instant of their eyes; at the intersection of those three tones of force I was transfixed as between spearheads as I talked. As I asked my questions, and told my purposes, and what I was looking for, it seemed to me they relaxed a little toward me, and at length a good deal more, almost as if into trust and liking; yet even at its best this remained so suspended, so conditional, that in any save the most hopeful and rationalized sense it was non-existent. The qualities of their eyes did not in the least alter, nor anything visible or audible about them, and their speaking was as if I was almost certainly a spy sent to betray them through trust, whom they would show they had neither trust nor fear of.[7]

Thus a passing inquiry may smell of danger and is not to be lightly made among simple people whose security rests in a natural knowledge of place and for whom the stranger opens the huge ambivalence toward him of fear and help. This is a visceral exchange. As the stranger approaches he is able to see more of the people on whom he imposes and they in turn read from his dress and bearing something of his intentions toward them. Between them there mounts the necessity of exchange long before any word is spoken. To tell all this would take so long and they, in any case, do not have the ability to articulate

7. Ibid., p. 33.

it. Thus Agee chooses to resolve the statement of their mutual relations and his relation to them through presenting them as statuesque figures, as though monumental in their sorrow and in their silence, molded by the pain of their labor, by the sparseness of their language, and above all in the way they stand over against the little part of the world and of human experience that belongs to them.

The third encounter that I want to describe arises out of Agee and Evans' coming upon a closed church that they want to enter. Again, the interest of this encounter is that it symbolizes the mystery of integrity and approach that throws back upon its spectator the look by which he seeks to inspect the secrets of persons and things.

> It was a good enough church from the moment the curve opened and we saw it that I slowed a little and we kept our eyes on it. But as we came even with it the light so held it that it shocked us with its goodness straight through the body, so that at the same instant we said **Jesus.** I put on the brakes and backed the car slowly, watching the light on the building, until we were at the same apex, and we sat still for a couple of minutes at least before getting out, studying in arrest what had hit us so hard as we slowed past its perpendicular.
>
> It lost nothing at all in stasis, but even more powerfully strove in through the eyes its paralyzing classicism: stood from scoured clay, a light lift above us, no trees near, and few weeds; every grain, each nailhead, distinct; the subtle almost strangling strong asymmetries of that which had been hand wrought toward symmetry (as if it were an earnest description, better than the intended object): so intensely sprung against so scarcely eccentric a balance that my hands of themselves spread out their bones, trying to regiment on air between their strengths its tensions and their mutual structures as they stood subject to the only scarcely eccentric, almost annihilating stress, of the serene, wild, rigorous light: empty, shut, bolted, of all that was withdrawn from it upon the fields the utter statement, God's mask and wooden skull and home stood empty in the mediation of the sun: and

> this light upon it was strengthening still further its imposal and embrace, and in about a quarter of an hour would have trained itself ready, and there would be a triple convergence in the keen historic spasm of the shutter.[8]

The sociological eye is caught in that which it sees because it is beholden to the community of the body's senses and its labors which stand out against time and the sky as the monuments of mankind. Thus every perception of ours belongs to the labor of man, fashioning himself and the legacy he leaves in his children. The church that stands against the sky is a symbol of the body's architecture and the shaping elements in the lives of the community that built it. The eyes that follow the contours of the church and upon entering take inventory of its furnishings cast the visitor's whole body into a reverent and mindful posture and thereby join him to the community in which he is at first a visitor or stranger. This is an experience that is repeated whenever we regard things with sociological concern: the disintegration or harmony we sense around us enters into us and determines our mood and purpose in the community. Thus the community shapes sociological concern at least as much as it is in turn molded by the ambitions of sociology. But we are forgetful of this in method, while at the same time proclaiming our factualism or realism. The truth is, however, that every object, like the church or the families encountered by Agee, is never a mere surface any more than the eye is the naked instrument of vision. We are caught in what we see and what we feel and the path to the things and persons around us is paved with the story of our own lives, without which there would be no bridges in the moment.

The wild sociologist is obsessed with trespass; for this is his access to the lives of others. In their third encounter Agee and

8. Ibid., p. 37.

Evans, still trying to break into the closed church, notice a young Negro couple walking by. They decide to ask them whether the minister can be found to let them in. Since the young couple are fifty yards or so ahead, Agee follows after them, his eyes taking advantage of their beautiful and buoyant bodies in a way that at a closer distance would be improper. For a brief moment, Agee is filled with the vision of the young woman, her young man—the sway of their bodies, how they are together—yet afraid all the time that his presence will startle them. Worse still, Agee is agonized lest his admiration be read as malicious intent through the young couple's misunderstanding of why he is coming up behind them. Suddenly, they startle, he calls after them, and they set off in a frightened run, more terrified as Agee in great anguish runs after them to plead that he meant no harm. The whole incident is a passing one and yet it is central to the consideration of the nature of trust implicit in the intrusions of social life. Every day we must penetrate the lives of others, interrupting their thoughts, or getting them to pause on their way, or to set aside their work for a moment. We do this from a thousand needs and not because we presume upon their help or mean to encroach upon others without consideration for them. For these reasons we need to trust to the rituals of approach even where, as sometimes happens, they do not quite succeed. At such times, I think we have to rely upon one another's experience to mend things. Agee fails to allow for this deeper trust in the young couple, perhaps a while later, to recover themselves and decide he meant them no harm. Thus, although he has the highest respect for the dignity of those whom he intrudes upon, Agee on this occasion in some sense denies them the judgment that experience brings in handling the inevitable misunderstandings that arise in human encounters. If Agee sins at all against the couple, it is because he does not allow for forgiveness from them. He insists upon being the greater victim of the misunderstanding, whereas the young couple, despite all the times they have been chased and beaten, might on this occasion have realized they had been startled and that it was their fear that set the other man after them because of his own anxiety not to be thought ill of by them. In short, there are some human encounters that can never be brought to account even though they are remembered by us and shape our conscience.

Wild sociology is not a solo effort. One might even say that it is not especially an affair of the heart, however it may seem to involve the emotions. Indeed, it is precisely because of the emotions involved that wild sociology is not properly alive in us unless it begins in the deepest trust toward others to understand and reciprocate the care we intend. Sociological care is not paternalism. It does not righteously diminish the responsible growth and variety of opinion that it will surely meet. It is not parasitic. Yet it is nurtured only in belonging to others. It seeks community without wanting to dominate the community. Sociological care is mutual; it remains active only in giving and being given life. Sociological care is not simpering. It is not exercised from empty need, or from loneliness. It is a musical response, a dance. Sociological care is not burdened. It does not work from obligation. Nor from guilt or any self-abasement. Wild sociology sings the world. Yet it always has a particular task, a local need, a definite work to do, not wasted in vain generality or empty intentions. Wild sociology never ceases to learn from what it believes it knows.

Wild sociology shoulders a common task. For this it is beholden to the world of everyday use, of custom, of trust, of invention, of hope and memory, and of the countless and immemorial repetitions of the human family, which has tilled and irrigated the fields, sailed seas, built towns, villages, and cities, which has woven wool and cloth, carved wood and stone, written books, made music, song, and dance, and all in so fine a tapestry that none of us can ever find the first thread. Wild sociology faces the seamless web of human activity in need of its own place and without any magisterial claim upon men's time. By contrast, scientific sociology is impatient for success. It seeks identity through domination. Thus it is tempted to usurp the unfinished task of community as the proper work of sociology, to manage it and divide it into the spoils of science. For this reason method and role are the idols of sociology's usurpation. They make of work an assured thing and of persons a transparent collective. In this way much is lost in favor of saving the possibility of sociology.

Wild sociology assumes the secularization of the redemptive tasks of humanity given in our care for one another, in our talk and listening, in the exchange of our labors. We have nothing that cannot be taken from us; everything we give needs to be received. We cannot live without welcome. This is the work of our frail divinity, which belongs neither to science nor to religion. It rests in the eye of God, which is the eye of love and the light of a compassionate world. Thus the family is the shelter of our concern and deserves more than anything the care of sociology. To accomplish this, sociology needs to set aside its noisy individualism and daytime ambitions, just as the family itself must gather into itself everything that separates and isolates it upon this earth.

> This family must take care of itself; it has no mother or father: there is no other shelter, nor resource, nor any love, interest, sustaining strength or comfort, so near, nor can anything happy or sorrowful that comes to anyone in this family possibly mean to those outside it what it means to those within it: but it is, as I have told, inconceivably lonely, drawn upon itself as tramps are drawn round a fire in the cruelest weather; and thus and in such loneliness it exists among other families, each of which is no less lonely, nor any less without help or comfort, and is likewise drawn in upon itself:
>
> Such a family lasts, for a while: the children are held to a magnetic center:
>
> Then in time the magnetism weakens, both of itself in its

tiredness of aging and sorrow, and against the strength of the growth of each child, and against the strength of pulls from outside, and one by one the children are drawn away:

Of those that are drawn away, each is drawn elsewhere toward another: once more a man and a woman, in a loneliness they are not liable at that time to notice, are tightened together upon a bed: and another family has begun:

Moreover, these flexions are taking place every where, like a simultaneous motion of all the waves of the water of the world: and these are the classic patterns, and this is the weaving, of human living: of whose fabric each individual is a part: and of all parts of this fabric let this be borne in mind:

Each is intimately connected with the bottom and the extremest reach of time:

Each is composed of substances identical with the substance of all that surrounds him, both the common objects of his disregard, and the hot centers of stars:

All that each person is, and experiences, and shall never experience, in body and in mind, all these things are differing expressions of himself and of one root, and are identical: and not one of these things nor one of these persons is ever quite to be duplicated, nor replaced, nor has it ever quite had precedent; but each is a new and incommunicably tender life, wounded in every breath, and almost as hardly killed as easily wounded: sustaining, for a while, without defense, the enormous assaults of the universe:

So that how it can be that a stone, a plant, a star, can take on the burden of being; and how it is that a child can take on the burden of breathing; and how through so long a continuation and cumulation of the burden of each moment one on another, does any creature bear to exist, and not break utterly to fragments of nothing: these are matters too dreadful and fortitudes too gigantic to meditate long and not forever to worship.[9]

Like all creative thought, sociological thinking needs the rhythm of night and day. This is because the sociologist is caught in the everyday involvements of his fellow men, using them without thought, presuming upon their mixed kindness,

9. Ibid., pp. 53–54.

cruelty, and indifference. Every day he is witness to the differences of wealth, strength, intelligence, compassion, and beauty that mark the parade of his fellow men, shaping their homes, their children, and the news they have of one another. The wild sociologist breathes these differences, making them into the pulse and rhythm of his own life and family. At the same time, he longs for the unity and embrace of mankind, for the sheltering care that harbors the particulars, faults, and injuries of human life. For this reason the night thoughts of the sociologist swarm around the windows of the little houses men have set like stars in the earth.

Every thought of ours seeks shelter from the journey it begins and in its course remembers how life began well, enclosed and protected in the embrace of home. All our adventures, imaginations, and dreams are nurtured in the bosom of home, and however far they lead us they remain in the circle of the homeward return. And somehow every observation of ours bears this same caress and is not an aimless looking nor an empty stare. We see things and others in the shaping circle of our intrusion and embrace; the weight of bodies, the paper on the walls, the lamps and chairs, the sounds of mealtimes, are never bare particulars but warm animal signs that attract us even though we stand off because they are not our home but half remind us. Thus in his heart the wild sociologist pays the price of knowledge in the truancy of childhood memories and moves among men in search of his right home and his true family, to which he has no title but the price of love and sorrow.

Concluding Sociological Prayer

How should sociology keep its place? After all, sociology is powerful, men are in need of it, and the world is increasingly the instrument of organization. Why should anything keep its place; what, after all, is **place** in a world that is "going places"? We are now so accustomed to change and growth that we scarcely stop to consider the sources that feed the stream of our life. Indeed, the modern world gives us our lives in such comfortable surroundings that the question of self and its circumstance is likely to remain a residual anxiety, aggravated perhaps by our political responsibility toward those on the margins of modern ease. Surely, sociology is a permanent institution. We have built it up beyond anything that need remind it of its poverty. Where sociology holds the mirror to nature how should it see itself?

The commonplace nature of wild sociology will not be easily understood. Thus many will read what I am saying and not find in it anything like sociology. My concerns will seem to answer to no concrete sense of the conduct of professional sociology. But the lack here does not lie in what I fail to say of that sort but in the reader's lack of any need to inspect what authorizes his own concrete version of sociology as something to be found or to be missed in his reading. Sociology is not a literal fact to be discovered apart from the circumstance of its approach or how it is we are alerted to what we have to reckon with in looking for sociology. The task is to find our sociological bearings. This is not a problem of method. It is a question of concentrating upon sociology the salvation of self and circumstance as a connection of love as well as of knowledge.

We sense who we are and where we are mostly to be found from local habit. Let us say we are sociologists; let them say we are philosophers. The philosophers will only smile. It is enough, in any case, that we have found a path along which we can think. For we must know where we are at home if ever we are to be able to look elsewhere. We cannot distinguish other ways or see other places unless we know our own. We must bear in ourselves the tension between our own spot and the places that are distant and strange. In this, our knowledge of good and evil is like the difference between home and away, between where we can be ourselves and where we cannot abide or dwell.

> ". . . Anything is one of a million paths [**un camino entre cantidades de caminos**]. Therefore you must always keep in mind that a path is only a path; if you feel you should not follow it, you must not stay with it under any conditions. To have such clarity you must lead a disciplined life. Only then will you know that any path is only a path, and there is no affront, to oneself or to others, in dropping it if that is what your heart tells you to do. But your decision to keep on the path or to leave it must be free of fear or ambition. I warn you. Look at every path closely and deliberately. Try it as many times as you think necessary. Then ask yourself, and yourself alone, one question. This question is one that only a very old man asks. My benefactor told me about it once when I was young, and my blood was too vigorous for me to understand it. Now I do understand it. I will tell you what it is: Does this path have a heart? All paths are the same: they lead nowhere. They are paths going through the bush, or into the bush. In my own life I could say I have traversed long, long paths, but I am not anywhere. My benefactor's question has

meaning now. Does this path have a heart? If it does, the path is good; if it doesn't, it is of no use. Both paths lead nowhere; but one has a heart, the other doesn't. One makes for a joyful journey; as long as you follow it, you are one with it. The other will make you curse your life. One makes you strong; the other weakens you."[1]

Circumstance, reason, and love, joined in bringing each of the particulars of our lives to their communal and historical fullness, accomplish the salvation of sociology. Yet in making sociology an extension of our love of circumstance we do not mean that it may not be nourished on a rough and harsh ground. For there is no love that does not till the ground of circumstance. Thus circumstantial love is not moved by things to our own perfection but is rather a love toward the perfecting of things and others that saves our first need of them in their universal connection and plenitude. It is a love to be found as much in our own gatherings as in the gatherings of things, and in both of these what is saved is the opening and light of the world in which we are reflected and multiplied like Adam in Paradise, or any man anywhere beholden to the life around him. Circumstantial love is the perfection of common need and its uses. This is not a matter of proving oneself but of belonging and beginning again, which is the commonplace of daily living. This ancestral place does not yield to those who hunt it; it does not lie in achievement or status. The commonplace is approached only in the widening circle of care.

In his doctrine of the commonplaces Aristotle treats dialectic and rhetoric as separable modes of intellectual and moral persuasion.[2] But such a separation is precisely what made sophis-

1. Carlos Castaneda, **The Teachings of Don Juan: A Yaqui Way of Knowledge** (New York: Ballantine Books, 1970), pp. 105–106.

2. Aristotle, **Rhetoric and Poetics,** trans. W. Rhys Roberts and Ingram Bywater (New York: Random House, The Modern Library, 1954); **Aristotle on Dialectic, The Topics: Proceedings of the Third Symposium Aristotelicum**, ed. G. E. L. Owen (Oxford at the Clarendon Press, 1968).

tic dialectic the intellectual pride and danger of Greek political life. For dialectic may persuade at the expense of the moral community to which it appeals, thereby undermining the true place of rhetoric. For these reasons Isocrates sought to make rhetoric service the ideals of **paideia,** that is, to correct the alternatives of intellectual arrogance and Platonic spiritualism with the commonplaces of community and nation.[3] In this manner Isocrates understood that rhetoric's own seat is its place within the life of the community whose discourse it strengthens in order, in turn, to draw upon it for its own special eloquence. Thus the commonplaces of rhetoric strengthen the communal art of memory and the associations of civic knowledge. For rhetorical style is the embellishment of the way of life that it reinforces and not simply a matter either of the speaker's character or of his topic.

Thus, to address sociology is not to deal in the personifications of a backward art. It is simply to suit our speech to its topic, which is the place of our communal life. What we seek to diminish or to embellish in the practice of sociology is addressed in terms of extreme alternatives in order to gather its tensions. For our aim is not the victory of a virtuous sociology any more than it is to refuse the temptations in the ordinary practice and institutions of sociology.

It may be asked, then, whether a sociology of the commonplace can be radical. I shall answer that in the face of the bureaucratic and corporate rationality of the professional sciences nothing can be more radical than a sociology inspired by the love of human circumstance and its great conventions. Wild sociology rejects the ambition of the professional social sciences to assimilate themselves to the structure of domination that teaches the oppressed to see themselves through the

3. W. W. Jaeger, **Paideia: the Ideals of Greek Culture,** trans. Gilbert Highet, 3 vols. (New York: Oxford University Press, 1939–1946).

eyes of their oppressors, to sift the oppressor's language for some word the people can understand, to accept as charity the return of their own gifts. This is not to deny that the social sciences may intend help, justice, and betterment. But these expectations have been promoted long enough now to leave the poor cynical toward those whose own lives are all that has benefited from our subscription to the social sciences. The danger in this is that practitioners of the sciences will find the lay community ignorant of the complexity of reform and thus rationalize lay hostility toward its practice even where the people's anger is reasonably grounded in the experience of disappointment and failure. For social reformers prefer to judge themselves by their own intentions rather than by the results of the institutions they bequeath to the poor.

Wild sociology encourages a way of looking at things and saying things that matures with its own practice. It presumes upon no hierarchy of men; it does not command the first word, nor does it insist upon the last word. It is found in a dialogue that is entirely rooted in the aspirations of human development and political community. Thus wild sociology cannot thrive where some have the right to speak and others only the obligation to listen. For in such a situation no one truly speaks and no one truly listens.

> Human existence cannot be silent, nor can it be nourished by false words, but only by true words, with which men transform it. Once named, the world in turn reappears to the namers as a problem and requires of them a new **naming**. Men are not built in silence, but in word, in work, in action-reflection.[4]

Without community, speech has no duty to listen for itself, to seek address, and to respond to those whose listening addresses their own self-inquiry and mutual need. True dialogue

4. Paulo Freire, **Pedagogy of the Oppressed,** trans. Myra Bergman Ramos, (New York: Herder and Herder, 1970), p. 76.

makes men and it is only men who are partners to dialogue. But such speech is impossible where there is no love of man and of the world he is called to think and say. Nor is this a sentimental love, for it is the bond of freedom and humanity against injustice, darkness, and oppression. Such a love therefore must know its enemies as well as its own weaknesses in order to fight oppression.

Wild sociology will encourage radicalism. Yet it will be hard on its own radicalism, suspecting further evils from its own activity should it presume upon its relation to the lay community. It may well be that the daily practice of sociology encourages arrogance upon the part of its members, undermining the very resources of humanism with a numb professionalism or the shrill cry of ideology. If this is not to happen wild sociology must make a place for itself, and to accomplish this it must engage hope and utopia. Hope is the time it takes to make the place in which men think and talk and work together. Thus wild sociology is essentially engaged in the education of the oppressed.

Sociology is nothing apart from its attachment to the world. It is for this reason that wild sociology must be mindful of its own spectacle. It cannot stand outside of the collective focus of seeing and being seen that is the natural light of man. In this light the world is our circumstance, the surround of things and others, the time they take, the places they inhabit, so that we are obliged to know their ways by living among them, shaping our own lives, our talk, and all our senses to their community. The task of wild sociology is not to collect the world for sociology. Wild sociology gathers only out and about in the world, in the epiphany of city, family, work, path, way, manner, face, child. It is a craft with nothing in hand but its own willingness to become a shape of community, a house of being.

Society is the great body of sociology. In this body the sociological eye is not the eye of the scientific observer but the eye of human divinity, the mystery of the care in the human look, its holy watch. Prior to synthesis or analysis the sociologist's look dwells upon the particularity and universality of each human being, of his moods, his places, and his works. This indwelling is a connection of the eye, the ear, the heart, and the mind of the sociologist in the great body of mankind that heals its own wounds in the strength of its time. The vision of wild sociology is a celebration, a responsibility, and a humble task no greater than a mother's care for her children or a father's labor, and is entirely unredeemed if it fails them in their patience, in their hope, and in their endurance. Its vision is beholden to its sense of mystery, its anger, its thirst for justice. In this, wild sociology is ambivalently suspended between self-purification and social reform, between revolution and unending predicament, between betrayal and forgiveness. For sociology is bewitched by a power of order, by the hope of some plan or design in which the lives of men and women will not seem fleeting occasions of the failure of humanity. And this expectation arises above all from the warm presence of human beings, from their ideas, hopes, and fears, which admit the sociologist without the cover of strangeness and alienation, however much these seize upon him in his watchful hours.

The wild sociologist means to keep faith with the great commonplaces of human life, birth, marriage, work, and death, and to be faithful to what is strange and varied, brave and defeated, in them. He must therefore learn to understand his own curiosity and not place it above its proper human concerns. For in the great body of mankind, in all its times and places, in all its beliefs and visions, the sociologist's own activity risks monstrosity in its pretended freedom and in its rootless possibility. Sociology is the poorest of the sciences, for it is brother to man unless it tricks him with the power of politics or the promise of history. Scientific sociology, however, is not always sure of its own work and is thus tempted by other enterprises as models of power and accumulation. These possibilities consume much of the energy of sociology in the effort to force its bread in the unseasonable factories of method. The way of ordinary men is infinitely more patient; it is repeated upon their lives in countless labors, monumental in the movement of fingers, eyes, and hands; in bending, lifting, folding, sowing, and cutting; in hauling, shipping, mining, flying, weaving, and baking; in watching, digging, planting, selling, and buying; in eating, drinking, sleeping, and living; in reading, writing, praying, and singing; in burying, marrying, mothering, and learning. And each of these is so finely wrought upon the bodies of men and women and of their children and families, in their homes and fields and in their factories, schools, and churches, in their markets, their streets and parks, that they are all so much music to the shaping circle of our being, our joy and sorrow—all in their endless epiphany.

It is in the midst of these things that are the world's blessing and instrument that we assume the common cares of sociology. For the concern of wild sociology is not just the encouragement of order in others but the very shape of our own life. It is for this reason that the commonplaces of social life are the occasions of our thanksgiving.

THE AUTHOR

John O'Neill is a graduate of the London School of Economics and Political Science and of Stanford University. He is now Professor of Sociology at York University, Toronto. He has lectured widely throughout the world and is an editor of the journals **Philosophy of the Social Sciences** and **The Human Context.** He is the author of **Sociology as a Skin Trade: Essays towards a Reflexive Sociology** and **Perception, Expression and History: The Social Phenomenology of Maurice Merleau-Ponty.** He has also translated Merleau-Ponty's **Humanism and Terror** and **The Prose of the World,** as well as Jean Hyppolite's **Studies on Marx and Hegel.** He is the editor of **Modes of Individualism and Collectivism** and the forthcoming **On Critical Theory.** He is presently working on **The Sociology of the Body.**